THE
BUMPER CARTOON BOOK

© Wolfe Publishing Ltd., 1970

© Daily Mirror Newspapers Ltd., 1970

SBN 723 40399 6

Printed photolitho in Great Britain by
Ebenezer Baylis & Son Limited
The Trinity Press, Worcester, and London

THE BUMPER

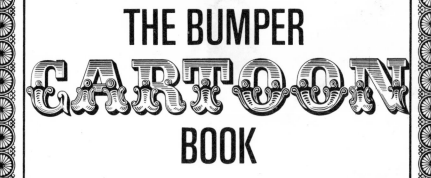

CARTOON

BOOK

*Over 3,000 cartoons from
the Daily Mirror*

WOLFE PUBLISHING LIMITED
10 EARLHAM STREET LONDON WC2

Contents

*For easy reference categories are listed in
alphabetical order*

"I think you're spoiling that dog."

"Go on behaving like this and you'll be sent down!"

"Take him for a proper walk — no wonder the poor thing's neurotic!"

"When I bought him you said he was fully grown!"

"Hide, you idiot, we're supposed to be extinct!"

"He's doing his best to help me get over poor Fido passing on."

"With a face like that,
it's about time you
learned to say
something besides
'Pretty Polly'."

"It's cruel the way they coop
those poor humans up."

"If I didn't bring him with me,
he wouldn't let me back in."

"What a lovely dog. Where does he live?"

"Let us imagine Inspector Maggs
is a cat stuck up a tree."

"Calm down, dear. There's a
perfectly simple explanation. . . ."

"You're spoiling that dog, Joe."

"Is it ALWAYS lovely wet weather like this, Mum?"

"That's the last time I give you dancing lessons!"

"Are you going to get in or do I have to throw you in?"

"He always likes to keep the children amused in some way"

"You'll have to speak up — my
ears are full of sand."

"Hundreds of cats in the pet shop
and I had to pick YOU!"

"You've done the crossword again!"

"Make up your mind — this isn't a Public Library!"

"O.K., I give up — WHAT has twenty legs and barks?"

"I don't know who's dog it is, but I wish people would feed their own animals."

"Sometimes I feel sorry I ever put him on this darn cat food."

"Whose flippin' idea was it to go out on the beer last night?"

"It's escaped!"

"I bet you can't do bird imitations."

"Good heavens, now they're checking on dog licences!"

"Poke me once more, mate, and you'll see what 'Joeykins' can do."

"She's a bargain for five bob. She's going to have puppies."

"We're dead worried about it. It's right off its food."

"THAT'S not a footprint, you clot!"

"Heel!"

"I suggest you take a couple of weeks off, Miss Jones — I think the work is beginning to tell on you!"

"He is pleased to see you!"

"Get me Perry Mason!"

"I think I preferred it when we had mice."

"We'll have to find another excuse to meet secretly."

"If you don't get off, I won't let you watch the dog-food commercials!"

"There must be OTHER ways of teaching him to be a good watch dog!"

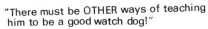

"You should see her first thing in the morning."

"Blimey! That worm must be putting up a hell of a fight."

"Uh-uh! — Seems it's going to be one of those days!"

"Mother thinks it's time I got
married and settled up."

"I wish they'd throw their crumbs on
the grass instead of on the concrete."

"G-r-r-r to you, too!"

"Alfie don't want any, he's just ate Elsie."

"You haven't bitten ANOTHER postman?"

"I've told you before, Henshaw, this happens to be a zoo, not a circus!"

"Bow wow!"

"Were YOU house-trained when YOU were two months old?"

"You go back to the zoo and tell them we want your redundancy payment in cash."

"To be brutally frank, madam,
little Sir Nigel of Netherington
is suffering from midriff bulge.

"Why did Rikki wag his
tail at that blonde?"

"We've made an unlucky start with
farming. The cow didn't give any
milk so we sold him!"

"About that lion you sent
to be stuff. . . . "

"His venom is very weak and his poor little crush-hold
is hardly a squeeze."

"Quack!"

"Can't you just BRING my slippers?"

"We've been invited to a budgie-swapping party."

"Well, YOU'RE no bird of paradise yourself."

"Good news, Chief — we caught her!"

"O.K. Let's see you eat THAT one!"

"It's scared stiff of flies, but it does keep the relations away.

"Boy! I'd hate to be you if anyone finds out about this!"

"It's nice to eat out for a change."

"Just you squeak when you're spoken to!"

"I was hoping we would be alone tonight."

"Who's next?"

"And a dog muzzle, please."

"I've heard they're marvellous roasted."

"What do you mean, you can't
tell the blokes from the birds?
The one in the middle is a dog."

"I have no statement to make . . . "

"By jove, isn't that a Syrian
mongoose-eating water python?"

" 'Ow abaht formin' a group?"

"Why don't we just buy a mousetrap?"

"Think yer'll be discovered by next week, son? 'Cos that's
when the electricity bill's due!"

"Stanley could be a great pianist if he wasn't left handed!"

"My boy likes to suffer when he sings."

"We've fixed you up with an engagement, Smilby — in the back of an ice cream van."

"Certainly he's got something . . . chuck him out before we all catch it!"

"Oops . . . beg pardon!"

"No wonder you can't get to sleep — you're round here half the night banging on my door."

"That's done it! — you've hit on the mating call of the yellow-nosed hornet."

"Watch out for these kids — I think I just signed a cheque!"

"Try to increase the aperture of your cakehole."

"Hells bells, Emily, why should we want television?"

"I'm from the top flat — we're trying to get some kip."

"Ha! So for all these years you've had no violin at all under there!"

"No, madam — there's nobody here murdering a cat!"

"Dunno whether to join the musicians' union or the woodworkers' union!"

"I gather that you play the piccolo, Mr. Mountebank."

"Just sing the song, we'll dub in the music later."

"Yes, her voice still charms the birds off the trees — they migrate quicker!"

" . . . Now don't forget I wrote this for massed brass bands and a choir of two hundred."

"One only, mate!"

"Who's the blonde? He's my manager, THAT'S who!"

"I can't find my mouth."

"Switch it off — I don't dig that trad stuff!"

"One moah time!"

"Eating peanuts during rehearsal again, Bagworth?"

"You haven't heard the worst yet — there's going to be a silver collection."

"Try for the trumpet-player now, dear."

"Senor Castiglione has never failed to play at a concert yet, and tonight will be no exception. . . ."

"Might I suggest a rather lighter model, sir?"

"I'll agree to a cease-fire if you will."

"Mother! Charlie was only going to tip the Taxi driver!"

"Other brides' fathers hire a car!"

"Saved by the bell, eh?"

"Important? Of course it's important — you want a honeymoon, don't you?"

"Couldn't we catch a later train, for Pete's sake?"

"You still haven't got over the crush you had on him, have you?"

"Surely you could have found somebody else to play in your place, just for tonight?'

"Well, what are YOU waiting for, a receipt?"

"Officer — this man keeps following me!"

"I think the bill for the reception is more than Daddy expected."

"They asked me if I was interested in trains, and I fell for it!"

"I see your friends over at the club are having their little joke!"

"Please, please . . . no confetti!"

B

"Really, Humphrey! You've simply RUINED what I wanted to be the smartest wedding of the season!"

"I always get married on the same date — it makes it easier to remember the anniversary."

"Smashing booze-up, what's it in aid of?"

"Sorry I'm late — they threw in an extra hymn."

"Blimey! You DO go off people quick, don't you?"

" D-Do you, Lionel Horatio (Yuk! Yuk!) Clarence (Heh! Heh!) FLOOP (Hee-Hee!) . . . ?"

"Where you off to then, love?"

"In a way I'm sorry you turned up, 'cos when the other two didn't, I got their helpings."

"They say the other girl took it pretty hard!"

"Her mother has always got to go one better!"

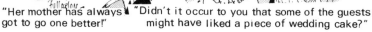

"Didn't it occur to you that some of the guests might have liked a piece of wedding cake?"

"Well, what excuse DID you make to your wife?"

"Couldn't I just give her away without having her gift-wrapped as well?"

"It's time you stopped objecting to my marriage, mother!"

"Will you explain that bit about worldly goods?"

"And what do you want to ask me a few questions about, Constable?"

"Hullo, darling! — I've done something today that I haven't done for AGES. . . ."

"As a matter of fact. Mr. Pilbright, I was just on my way round to the church!"

"Didn't expect me to leave it at the reception for your relations to finish off, did you?"

"You don't mean to say you want to be cooped up inside a stuffy old church on a lovely day like this!"

"A rise, Finlay? By golly, your wife hasn't wasted much time, has she!"

"I distinctly told you — NEXT Saturday!"

"Not that vintage! I've been saving that for a special occasion!"

"I claim sanctuary . . ."

"What did you put on those invitations, Daphne?"

"Cut the delivery a bit fine haven't you?"

"This was my first wedding and I'm still trying to think where I went wrong!"

"Jolly good show, mum!"

"Of course I still love you!"

"This is the oddest blind date I've ever been on."

"I do."

"Just a touch of nerves."

"This just isn't my day!"

"It was just going to be a quiet wedding — then her husband got to hear about it!"

"Well if you're just making friends with the neighbours, I suppose it's all right."

"Drop in and see the boys at the Red Lion when the gilt has worn off, Joe."

"It's his fourth marriage."

BLOGFORD FOOTBALL CLUB

"You know, Skip, I still think it's only SHIP'S captains who can do it!"

"It's all right for you single chaps — you've only got yourselves to think about. I could come with you, tomorrow, though!"

"Does that 'Forsaking all others' include the Queen's Head Darts Team?"

"Dad! Uncle Bert! At last we've got someone to do the washing up!"

" 'Let him now speak, or forever hold his peace!' Was that loud enough?"

REX

"Hold it, Frilby! You'll swoop when I tell you to swoop!"

"All the book says is 'No smoking and no drinking whilst on duty'"

"Is this man pestering you, Miss?"

"And you are requested to make no attempt to leave the neighbourhood until our inquiries are completed."

"Am I right in assuming this is your first plain-clothes assignment, Constable?"

"Once upon a time . . . "

"Up to now, Higgins, we've been pretty lenient . . . "

"Never been the same since 'e took the dog-handling course!"

" . . . and furthermore, madam, impersonating an officer."

" . . . This is Constable 496 Wittering, in the boot of the getaway car . . . we seem to be in some sort of automatic car park over."

"I think you'll have to face it, son — if your Mum had wanted you back, she'd have collected you by now."

" . . . proceed immediately to . . . "

"All right you two, move along!"

"I suppose you're wondering what a nice girl like me is doing in a place like this."

"You're all right, Sir, but I'm afraid we will have to take the horse away for further tests!"

"That looks suspicious — the Mint with a hole in it."

"I like the idea of giving them a sporting chance."

"It's lucky for you lot that you can give a reasonable explanation of why you're here."

"You can't speak to him without a search-warrant."

"Now, then, Sir, what makes you think someone's out to get you?"

"The Commissioner of Police? I'm SO pleased to meet you. And how are things down at the 'nick'!"

"Just some routine questions, Mr. Smith."

"Give 'em my love, mate!"

"Me occupation, Sarge?
Company Director."

"We are police officers!"

"No! Not you!"

"Dad's not going to like this, Ma!"

"You said, 'Take him down to the station to make a statement', — and he did he said 'Goodbye'."

"I get fed up patrolling the same boring route, night after night . . ."

"Come on out, Bugsy — we know you're in there!'

"Now probably clean-shaven. Uses many aliases."

"No you don't — you sit in the back!"

"I think it was suicide."

"Excuse me, sir, are you a lover?"

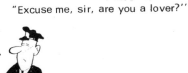

"Why, Herb Trimble! What brings YOU out on a night like this?"

"Would you like to ask Bonnie to tune it down a bit, Clyde?"

" . . . nobody is to leave this room!"

"It's Reveille, General."

"Midnight bathing on duty is
NOT encouraged, Bixby . . . "

DICKENS

SHOES

LIZ

"Now put down: 'I was proceeding along Hall Lane on my
bicycle when' . . . "

"All right, Johnson, for the last time — what have you done with the light bulbs?"

"D'you mind — I'm trying to sleep!"

"Hold it! — That's the Chief Inspector you've got there!"

"You can't take him, he was a wedding present!"

"All right you, move along!"

"Before you say anything, Sarge, I must warn you that the chips are soggy!"

"Officer! This man is annoying me."

"Well, well! Blowed if it isn't Fred Bloggs — King of the Shoplifters!"

"Stolen car . . . Duotone, Jasmine White, Peach Blossom Pink . . . Morning Mist Upholstery . . . "

"Fingerprints can't lie, Sergeant!"

"Proceed, Stebbings! Don't walk, lad — proceed!"

"Any clues as to why your wife may have left home, sir?"

"About those three dummies you stripped — one of them happened to be Miss Friday."

"Sorry, sir. We don't open until tomorrow."

"Oh why don't you wrap up?"

"We don't SELL anything, we just give stamps . . ."

"I think it's time we tackled this problem of shoplifting seriously."

"Actually our trading figures are well down, but it's been a terrible week for shoplifting . . ."

"Some people just can't take a hint!"

"How would one go about setting a school on fire please?"

"I'd like to see some linoleum, please!"

"No wonder we haven't had a single customer today — you forgot to unlock the doors."

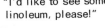

"See what I mean?"

"I KNOW! I KNOW! I use one of the same make myself!"

"Psst! What time did 'Complaints' start work this morning?"

"Where shall I put it?"

"What makes you think this lady's been shoplifting?"

"Thirty years ago I was in furs and silk lingerie — but we all come to it, dearie!"

"We've run out of trading stamps, lady. . . ."

"Is there an easier way to take the lids off your tins?"

"You're not looking too well, Miss Perkins — take a card and go and lie down!

"Had a terrible morning, dear . . . something wrong with a new treacle-tart we're selling."

"Mr. Ogalik here will be taking over the frozen food department."

"No, fatty. We have no complaints department."

"Yes?"

"Don't bother keeping your eye on her — she's the decoy. . . ."

"Will I criticise the service on the food counter? — Will I complain about your shoddy nylons? — Don't miss tomorrow's thrilling episode!"

"I wish to complain about the amount of starch you've been putting in my collars!"

"And another thing, Alice, when people ask about my job, don't say I'm an informer!"

"Now, look here, Jackson. . . ."

"I think you'd better make a few changes here, Harcourt!"

"I think it must be some electrical fault."

"Watch her, Hoskins, I don't like the way she's eyeing those powder compacts!"

"Sorry, madam, we're sold out — we had three lighthouse keepers in here this morning."

"You know too much."

"Who said anything about handkerchiefs shrinking? — These are double sheets!"

"Stand by your beds."

STOP ME & BUY ONE

"Mr. Johnson, you're supposed
to contemplate your own navel."

"But you can't **all** be away the last week in August."

"Smile, please!"

"I think he wants a tip."

" . . . and try not to cause another run on Sterling."

" . . . and if you put the policy in your wives' names, on your death, they will each receive 39s. 4d . . . "

HIGH CLASS JEWELLERS

. . . a quarter of assorted diamonds please."

SCHOOL FOR SNAKE CHARMERS

"I'm dreading Christmas — last year they ALL gave me after-shave lotion!"

"This sort of thing's going to KILL us small shopkeepers!"

"Now this is one of our more interesting stock-taking jobs."

"Like to come out for an English meal tonight?"

" — and stop disappearing when I'm talking to you!"

"You've got a flat, sir!"

"Look, Dad — an Indian!"

"I tell you, I was swatting flies — not bidding!"

"If I'd known what they meant by a charm school . . . ".

" . . . an everyday story of country folk . . . "

"I suppose you think that's funny, do you?"

"I owe you an apology, sir — I've lost the pay-roll."

"We should never have started that 'Send no money' advertisement!"

"Throw him back in here, Miss McGlinsky — there's something I forgot to say."

"There's a time and a place for everything, Harris — but I see you've discovered that!"

"Better call me 'Sir' — it wouldn't do for people to know that my wife works."

"Rutherford may crack under pressure, but his loyalty to the firm is unquestionable."

"Old J.B. can be pretty rough if your sales are below target."

"Sounds like Doreen — no doubt with some fantastic excuse for being late again."

"Just had Chobley in here. Asked for a rise and when I said NO, he fell grovelling at my feet."

"I've been expecting you!

"Miss Jones — why is it I always get the broken biscuits and the cup with a chip in it?"

HEAD BUYER

c

"When was it you sent in this request for a raise, Simpkins?"

"Not ANOTHER of those damn industrial espionage agents?"

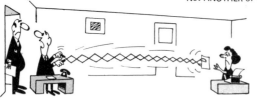

"She's got a shocking cold."

"I thought you were supposed to be working with a skeleton staff!"

"I've been back two weeks now and I think it's time you forgot that blonde temporary."

"Watch out, he's a proper Casanova! Dammit, he's even made a pass at ME!"

" . . . and I can assure you that the strength of our product is exceptional . . . "

"Good morning, Miss Bennet — take a letter!"

"Did you HAVE to duplicate and circulate that note I'd slipped in about our weekend at Brighton?"

"My typxwritxr's gonx wring."

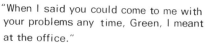

"When I said you could come to me with your problems any time, Green, I meant at the office."

"She's a programme girl in the computer section."

"Empty that at once!"

"Simpkins has got a nerve going sick — he knows it was my turn to have 'flu."

"I must get my watch fixed. This is the second time I've been early this week."

"Mr. Jones, sir, come to see about his rise . . . "

"Promotion's ruddy slow here, mate
— takes ten years to get
a desk of your own."

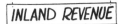

"Miss Smith . . . please tell me that one day
you'll appear on my claim allowances!"

"Yes — I could learn how to feed a
computer — what do they eat?"

"Coffee and biscuits are a bit late this
morning, aren't they?"

"Dash it all, Smithers — why can't you
bring your lunch in a brief case?"

"Mr. Watson doesn't want
to see ANYONE today!"

"Miss Findike, when I said 'Throw him out' I really meant through the door!"

"According to our industrial espionage section, sir, Sprongle's Chairman uses an interlocking grip."

"Hey! What about a reference?"

"O.K. Jock — the office collection's gone up to the next floor!"

"If that's about more heat in your office again, Wickes . . . "

"On a clear day you can actually see through the windows."

"Really, Mr. Fenwick, is this a
follow-up to your inquiry
of the 9th inst . . . ?"

"Even if he IS a friend of yours, we
can't send him a letter ending
'Yours faithfully, J. D. Blooper and
Cuddles'!"

"I'll find Mr. Little's letter as quick
as I can — there's an awful lot of
'Misters'."

"The letter you wrote to our Leeds
branch — they've sent
it back to be decoded."

"But you got a rise in your
pay-packet last week. Didn't
your wife tell you?"

"Thinking of you? —
OF COURSE I'm thinking of you!"

"I've been with the firm ten years
and I've never got to know the boss!"

"Must dash — I'm late for work
and it's nearly my lunch hour."

"Would you mind tasting my coffee, Miss Jenkins? I hear one
of the staff has won the pools today . . . "

" . . . and kindly stop referring to it as the gas-chamber."

"I said read it back to me not backwards!"

"We also have a very generous discontinued bonus scheme . . . ."

"I KNOW it's no use asking for a rise these days, sir, but I was wondering what you do with your cast-off clothing."

"You'd better re-type this list, Miss Formby, you've spelt redundancies' wrongly."

"He certainly doesn't need THAT!"

" . . . and this time I'm going to DEMAND a raise!"

"I won't tell you again — this fighting must stop!"

"What do you think of the new boss?"

"I know I said we were one big, happy family here, Smithson, but don't keep calling me Dad!'

"I thought putting your pin there might possibly have more results, Smedly!"

"He calls it 'delegating responsibility' — I call it passing the buck!"

"That reminds me — your dentist says it's time you had a check-up . . ."

"To show our appreciation of your work, the directors have awarded to you a personal bicycle space on the company's parking lot!"

"At last I've managed to get out of my rut — they've sacked me!"

"You're home, dear. The nasty boss can't get you now!"

"Duxbak Roofing Company, can I help you?"

"Have you any idea what the meeting's been called for?"

"Might I suggest you try it for thump, Mr. Biddle?"

"This is Mr. Schenk, our production manager. Mr. Schenk has been very naughty. Listen to what Daddy is going to say to naughty Mr. Schenk."

"Poor Mr. Williams — keeps standing there, hoping the boss will come out and ask him for a light."

"As my wife handles the money in our family, Sir, why shouldn't she discuss my raise with you?"

" — and don't forget to insist on a pension!"

" 'Semicolon' — is there a hyphen in that?"

"The 'pleasant working conditions'?
— Here she comes!"

"Marvellous character references, and from four different weighing machines too!"

"Mark this one urgent. 'Dear Sir, re your bottle of the seventeenth last . . . '"

"No — YOU tell me your name
— then I tell you if he's in!"

"Sorry I'm late for dinner, dear.
I overslept at the office."

"I've had complaints that the rest
of the staff find you
very unapproachable."

"Of course, you'll have to
shave that beard off."

"This my TEMPORARY secretary,
Major — my wife hasn't seen
her yet."

"Yes, Mr. Winthrop is free
at dawn tomorrow."

"Mr. Henderson, you're wanted on the phone."

"He's generally in a good mood between his mid-morning depression and after-lunch hangover, if you can find it!"

"Wake up, dear — we're at the station."

"Just remember that I'M the head of this company!"

"Managing Director or not, if you WILL come to the office so early . . . "

"Fired? I always thought slaves were sold!"

"Be sure you're not working when he arrives, then he'll think I'm out!"

"Sir — ninety three point five per cent of our staff want more money."

"I can never tell whether Dobson is overworked, too slow, or absent."

"Don't overdo it, Fanshaw, there's still the other foot."

"Oh, hello, darling . . . OF COURSE I still love you. I always will . . . What? Oh, nothing much . . . just taking some dictation . . ."

"Can I ring you back, dear?"

"Now watch it — I've got friends in high places!"

"Not bad, eh? — For a man who's been brought back out of retirement!"

"Hello, boss. Like to hear my baby gurgling?"

"There's no point in waiting to catch him in a good mood — this IS his good mood!"

"And here's a copy of the company song, which may be hummed, but not whistled, during working hours!"

"His references from the Duke of Suffolk and the Eari of Leicester seemed very impressive until I found out they were pubs."

"When I've had too much I see everything in triplicate!"

"Henry has a most important job — he's the one who gets all the blame."

"I'll say the notice has had an effect on the staff! Half of them have left to get better jobs.

"You CAN'T sack him — he doesn't work here!"

"Come back you idiots! I said 'They've put a man into ORBIT not AUDIT'."

"Something's gone wrong
with the holiday rota, sir."

"You're very touchy this
morning, Miss Hammond!"

"We just changed the directions on the
bottle from 'Use Sparingly'
to 'Use Liberally'."

"It amazes me why he doesn't marry
her and get himself a new secretary!"

"Remember that 'Money back if not
satisfied' offer? Well, they're NOT!"

" . . . 3, 2, 1! One hour to go . . . 59, 58, 57 minutes . . . "

"He's engaged!"

"Huh! Too ill to come to work all week — but well enough to come in on pay day!"

"Got off on the wrong floor yesterday and spent the entire day working for some dam'n firm I've never heard of."

"Catch ME wearing a see-through blouse!"

"O.K., so it can be done — but what does it prove?"

"Have a chat with that little blonde widow in the spotted dress, George. She's probably lonely."

"O.K.! Who's the comedian who dumped all the empties around mother?"

"Don't be silly, Gladys — your parties are ALWAYS lovely!"

"Hold it!"

"You're standing on my husband!"

"This is something in the nature of a brand new venture for the social club, sir."

"Angela! Just hand the olives around in HERE."

"I can't help it, Gladys — it's that after-shave lotion you bought me!"

"Hurry up, Phyllis — they're judging the Fancy Dress Contest at nine o'clock!"

"Actually, madam, I'm a Doctor of PHILOSOPHY!"

"Your autobiography was so thrilling — DO write another!"

"She's got quite a story to tell — if you give her half a chance."

"Let's go — it's getting dull!"

"But I CAN'T go to bed —
Mr. Stenwick's in it. . . ."

"Don't give Mr. Ramsey any more
to drink — that's his wife
he's chasing!"

"That must have been some
party last night, Fred."

"Try to look glamorous — here
comes my ex-wife."

"Now let's talk about YOU — tell me
what you think of my new dress."

"Hey nonny NO!

"He wasn't very good at
Postman's Knock. . . ."

"My husband came down half an
hour ago to complain about the
noise . . . "

"Here's someone to listen to you."

"Gentlemen of the jury, have you reached a verdict?"

"Bang goes another old saying . . . !"

"Then his lordship said 'So you have no fixed abode? — We can soon fix THAT!'"

"I got on great, the judge gave me twelve months in Holloway."

"Here, take my card in case you need me again some time!"

"You're not helping your case by addressing me as 'Madam Chairman'!"

"We find the defendant just a teeny-weeny bit guilty!"

"And is it not a fact, Mr. Frisby, that ever since the hospital gave you the wrong injections, you cannot obtain employment except as a hat-rack . . . ?"

"You realise that this is going to be a tough rap to beat?"

"I'm hearing a SHOCKING case at the moment — a man dressed up as a woman."

"Very nice, Mrs. Murgatroyd — but as your solicitor, my advice is to plead guilty and pay the parking fine!"

"You're not at the Old Bailey now, you know — and I say Jimmy DIDN'T spill the milk!"

"You say you were shopping early for Christmas — suppose the Beak asks why you didn't wait till the shop opened?"

"Then my lawyer said, morally you've won the case — legally you've got fifteen years."

"Yes, this is the gun I accidentally shot my poor dear wife with."

"Don't underestimate us, Millbright. We have ways of teaching you to talk."

"The formula from a top Civil Servant is in our hands! 'First warm the pot . . . '"

"Goodbye Carstairs — and good luck!"

"M.I.5. Disguise Department
— Miss Wilkinson speaking."

"It's my private eye."

"Fancy some microfilms for afters, Boris?"

"Hurry it up, James — I told my Mom I'd be back home by ten . . . "

"I told you to observe the radar installations, comrade, not the nudists' beach!"

"We've had a warning that the room might be bugged."

"This, gentlemen, is the earliest known bugging device."

"He worked for M.I.5."

"Open wide please . . . "

"It's very quiet — time somebody nicked the Goya again."

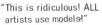

"This is ridiculous! ALL
artists use models!"

"Just now and again, Mr. Easel, do you think I might have the rent in cash?"

"Did I ever tell you about my operation, dear?"

D

"It's not their fault, officer — my stuff is very controversial."

"Brilliant, my boy! May I buy it?"

"Yes, I love it, I LOVE it — but where are the clues?"

"Now, Miss Gooseflesh you remember the pose you took yesterday . . . ?"

"Most of his friends have gone commercial, but not my Arthur!"

"The signature's good."

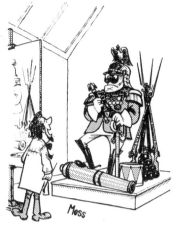

"Smile, please."

"When you asked me to model for you, you didn't say it was for a gargoyle."

"That reminds me — how about fixing the kitchen tap?"

"I'll say THIS for it — it'll never be stolen."

"Quick, tell him another one — he's stopped laughing."

"I've been commissioned
to design a new pillar-box!"

"How's the design for the new
stamp coming along?"

"Who said anything about painting?
I just want to look at you!"

" . . . and then I thought to
myself, what can I put in the
exhibition this year?"

"I'll NEVER get the cleaning
done at this rate, sir!"

"Sorry, Miss Carter . . . I should
have warned you about the
electric fire behind that screen!"

"They want you to do an encore — somebody's still got some tomatoes left."

"Ah! They don't write songs like that any more!"

"You didn't throw 'em that hard before we were married!"

"Close your eyes, girls — I'm coming in to fix the tap!"

CHORUS DRESSING ROOM

RED ARMY DANCERS

"I wish political asylum."

"... Let's face it, darling — you've toured for so many years as 'Snow White' they're beginning to call you 'Brand X' ..."

ROLO THE CONTORTIONIST

"They say he talks about himself behind his back!"

GRAND PANTOMIME MOTHER GOOSE   No 1 DRESSING ROOM

"See what I mean? — He's got typed."

"Sorry, girls, but a gimmick ain't everything you know!"

"Elsie, I've changed my mind about volunteering for this lark."

"Hello! That the Lonely Hearts Bureau?"

(a) "You'll have to wait while I dress,"

(b) "You can come in now."

"What a business to go bust in."

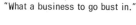

" . . . we'll call you."

"What else do you do?"

"Oh, no! Not ANOTHER family troupe."

"The dog isn't really talking — the parrot's a ventriloquist!"

"The part of the Welshman has been filled — the Dai is cast, you might say."

"I'm fed up with appearing in crowd scenes!"

"Hurry up with my ad-libs boys — I've got to do an encore."

"Ladies and Gentlemen, may I have your attention please?"

"Mooooooo . . . "

"Great performance, lads — pity this is the wrong theatre."

"Oh — it's just a stage he's going through!"

"Come OUT of there — it isn't our turn yet!"

"Two pints please, milkman!"

"I didn't read the small print in my contract!"

" . . . and now, ladies and gentlemen — Marvo, and his performing blasted dogs!"

"Dear Ardent Fan: Enclosed please find a lock of my hair as requested . . . !"

"I enjoyed the play, what was it like in the bar?"

"We can't wait for him — who's next?"

"Before you go on, darling, there is just ONE small point — we're doing Madame Butterfly tonight!"

"Don't forget to tell Aunt Agatha she was wrong — there's no sign of oil on the beach."

"Still, we're gradually getting the hang of the lingo, Basil."

"Bad news dear — I've just been looking at those forms I signed, and we're not on a six-week holiday cruise — we're emigrating!"

"If it wasn't for this wretched credit-squeeze, we'd be spending the winter on the Costa Brava!"

"MY hubby started his holiday, too!"

"George, dear, it's the window cleaner!"

" . . . And if we'd gone to Spain you'd be moaning about the heat and the flies . . . !"

"back at the office. I'd be having a lovely cup of tea right now."

"Psst! I tell you he'll whip you round the cemetery, round the gas works, back to the sewage outfall and you've had it."

"Well, the ad. definitely said it sleeps seven."

"But you've got to admit, Gladys, we've never had the beach all to ourselves like this in July."

"Remember, Fred, when we used to gaze into each other's eyes on the beach like that?"

" . . . and that's my poor, dear wife again. Naturally, I thought that Thing was only after her ice-cream cornet."

"NOW what do we do for spending money?"

"English economy wing? . . . First on your left!"

"But how can you have blisters already? We've only walked down the garden path."

"It's a terrific sensation —
I feel like a swallow!"

"Just think, Joe, if it wasn't for all that
beastly rain we could be enjoying a nice
healthy stroll down the prom."

"Just keep digging and you'll find
some yellow stuff called sand!"

"I don't think my husband trusts me."

"Rain is nature's watering can — without it,
there would be no pretty flowers, no pretty
grass, no pretty trees, no pretty . . ."

"A beach to ourselves is all very well,
but I hope your friend remembers to
collect us this evening!"

"They certainly don't leave much road for cyclists!"

"By the time we get to the water with this lot on, I'll be too tired to swim."

"Well, at least we'll be able to go straight in swimming after THIS lunch!"

"Penny for the guy, mister?"

"I told you a month was too long to leave the plants!"

"Sounds good – got a picture of the Captain?"

"I told you the travel allowance
wouldn't last five minutes."

"Not many people know
of this picnic spot."

"Shouldn't that read: 'Have you anything left'?"

"Where do I plug in the electric blanket?".

"Why can't you relax, Arthur, instead of coming down to the beach dressed up?"

"Me Jane."

"What do you mean, ANOTHER lousy Monday morning? You're on holiday!"

"Muriel — your tan has cost me ten bob a square inch."

"For heavens sake turn over Tom, and stop breathing down my neck like a horse!"

"No, sir, Beachley Holiday Camp
is five minutes up the road!"

"He seems to have
taken quite a fancy to Daphne."

"Back again from Bognor?"

"... and it's only a few
minutes from the sea."

"Our summer holiday
has arrived, dear."

"We guarantee you will be truly
amazed when you see the open
plan chalet, the secluded
aspect, and built in fridge!"

"Cigarettes, chocolates,
ices, sea air."

"What if we did take the wrong road?
Where's your gipsy blood?"

"When you've memorised
the route swallow it."

"First fine day since we've been here, so we're out making the best of it!"

"Two weeks of the best years of my life I've given you. . . ."

"Welcome to sunny Brightsea — and please don't leave wet umbrellas, raincoats and galoshes in the bedroom."

"My husband has taken up a most unusual hobby."

"Correct me if I'm wrong, but do you advertise this place as a home from home with no restrictions, or not?"

"Here's an interesting bit . . . did you know that Britain has over 3,000 miles of coastline?"

"That place is no good — the last time I left my wife there, she found her way back within a week."

"The only one he managed to get straight is the Leaning Tower of Pisa!"

"Good old waterproof watch! . . . Ten minutes to opening time!"

"Do you know, dear, you can see
5 television regions from up
here!"

"Well, you should insist they give you your fortnight in
summer like everyone else."

"Oh, stop complaining, George!
It's not Grandad's fault the
donkeys aren't here this year."

"I suppose we can be thankful for one thing . . . it's eased up
considerably since last week!"

"What do I do? . . . pay by the inch?"

"Something real he-manish, Miss —
I don't want geezers gettin'
the wrong idea."

"May I help you, ma'am?"

"I knew it! They've charged for the baby again!"

'ee . . . something tempting, with a hint of moonlight and roses."

"Isn't that the chap who told us he was a liver and kidney specialist?"

"It couldn't be much fresher, madam, I only ran over it this morning."

"What a marvellous offer, Dudley remind me to buy a dog on the way home!"

"Don't tell me! — You've been to that. ruddy antique shop aga . . . "

"Well, don't just SIT there — get an evening job . . . "

"No, Henry, we're NOT home yet — we're still in Harridges!"

"I'm just the same, can't manage to save a penny these days!"

"It's too expensive — I'll wait until you have your sale."

"How much of that nice pink flex would it take to knit an electric blanket?"

"Er, no — he smells like that already."

"Not bad, eh? Considering it was early closing day."

"Fred! — Have you eaten all that liver yet? Only I can't find those stick-on soles I bought."

"Some free gift! — Wrapping paper and string!"

"That insurance policy's a real bargain — you ought to break your leg more often!"

"I can picture you now, sir, breakfast in bed every morning!"

"Can I hear this one, please?"

"Now what else is there? Oh, yes, dog biscuits."

"Just popping out for fags, love.

" . . . and ½lb of butter!"

"See that, dear?"

"Yes, darling!"

"That's just how my tongue felt when I got up this morning."

"Her shoes are size 5, if that's any help!"

"Why shop there if you
don't trust them, Edna?"

"Last week's steak was fine,
I'm still wearing it!"

"But, darling, I NEEDED these
things, there were two empty
hangers in my wardrobe!"

"15/- over. That all right?"

"Ai'm afraid half-a-crown's worth
would be practically inaudible."

"Watch it, Miss! — You've put
HIM on my bill!"

"How are we going to make a four at solo now that Fred's run off with my wife?"

"HOUSE!"

"This was my full house at the Palais Dance-hall, this is a line at the Royal Theatre and this was my jackpot win at the Rovers Football Ground."

"He's fainted — pop out and get him some fresh air, somebody."

"For goodness sake, Alfred — nobody's trying to look at your cards!"

"I came away with a small fortune today — trouble is, I started with a BIG one!"

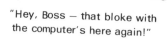

"Hey, Boss — that bloke with the computer's here again!"

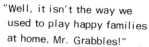

"Well, it isn't the way we used to play happy families at home, Mr. Grabbles!"

"All right — you beat him at snap!"

"If you can't be a good loser, don't play!"

"She'll do anything to scrape an acquaintance!"

"Smithy's certainly gambling the lot on this hand!"

"Maud's got another bingo session tonight so she's getting in a bit of practice . . . !"

"Having a bad day at Kempton Park isn't a good enough reason for joining."

"Looks like Fred's had another hot tip."

"What's the point of backing it each way? — They don't run there and back!"

"Honestly, I'm hopeless at all this What d'you call these black-currant shaped things again?"

"Let's make this the last hand — I want to watch Double Your Money!"

"Not only have I been drinking, Alice, but I have won Bert Higg's wife at poker."

"Which shirt do you want back?"

"See if you can get the pin in the PAPER this time, Ethel!"

"Now, Henshawe, I don't mind you running the occasional office sweepstake, but . . ."

"People like that are a constant drain on the National Health."

"I'd like to report my wife missing — as from tomorrow."

"Ah! It's how he'd have wanted to go!"

"I knew you'd soon come creeping back to apologise!"

"What's happened to everybody?"

"The natives seem restless tonight, don't they, Ron?"

"I think I'd better get Henry's dinner ready."

"I told you so, Harriet!"

"Isn't it about time you got used to this 'phone ringing, Ethel?"

"I think you had better let them pin their own flags on!"

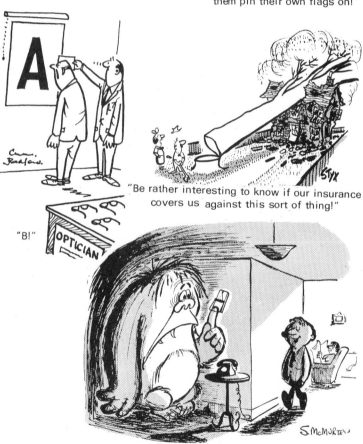

"Be rather interesting to know if our insurance covers us against this sort of thing!"

"B!"

OPTICIAN

"Sounds as if we've caught that ruddy mouse at last."

"I've slipped! Pass it on!"

"Not to worry — ! can't swim."

"It's the last time I try my hand at home-made bread!"

" — Five — Four — Three — Two — . . . "

"What're you sighing for?"

"Reg, don't keep asking
me to let you out —
I tell you, I've
lost the key!"

"Can you spare
a minute?"

"How about a drop of the hard stuff?"

"Say! Charlie certainly
can yodel can't he?"

"You want an 'eavier stone than THAT, mate!"

" . . . what exactly DID you say to him, Henry?"

"You're not expecting supper, are you?"

"Something's worrying you, dear, I can sense it!"

"Go on — I bet you say that to ALL the girls."

"Fred, we sold the houseboat — remember?"

"Three days ago, you promised
to send a plumber. . . ."

"See you Friday, then, Alf . . .
all being well. . . ."

"We wuz robbed!"

"Right,then — that's Lofty for the main gate, you, Spike, for the watchman an' Trixie to keep the guard dog occupied."

"Well, Luigi, we haven't come to wish you many happy returns."

"What is it this time — shoplifting, robbery with violence, or the same old juvenile delinquency?"

"One of them was a girl in a red mini-mini skirt — didn't notice what she looked like . . . "

"It's just that I've got this thing about being punctual . . . "

"Take yer stocking off, nut!"

"I got the tip-off they've installed some new-fangled safety device."

"Trust a clot like you to take the wrong turning!"

"Why, Mr. Pilson! How are things at the Bank?"

"The trouble is, it takes AGES to clear the words up afterwards."

"Fill 'em both up!"

"That bleedin' laundry! This is the third bullet-proof vest they've ruined!"

"Stick 'em up, Sir."

"Right, lads! Now when I give the signal, we go over the top and inside!"

"I thought you meant I could choose my present at a SHOP!"

"Now, remember, Louis, shoot first an' ask questions after."

"Meantersay yer never 'eard that supersonic bang?"

"Er, wot time you want the job done, boss?"

"Y'know, Fred, you haven't much time left to think up a story for the Christmas Club members."

"Like to pay our last respects to Big Louie."

"Are you sure it was only a parking offence, George?"

"Big Louie ain't dead!"

"I'll never know why you didn't hand it over when the police gave you the chance."

"Mind if we wait?"

"Wot's all this abaht you beltin' orf tickets for the Police Ball?"

"No, I'm not expecting him back tonight."

"Drop this in at the butcher's, Jim. I'll only need one now."

"It's not the police — it's the Inland Revenue, they've heard we're making a bomb!"

"Shall I stack 'em in the 'Out' tray, pro tem?"

"And they said it couldn't be done!"

"Some burglar! You can't even come in without waking the baby!"

"Three returns and one single!"

"Now I suppose I'll 'ave to resign from all me clubs . . . "

" 'Ow did wot 'appen?"

"Well, I think it's a lousy retirement plan."

"You KNOW it's tomorrow we draw our pensions, son."

"In case you're skint, my special offer this week is ten bob down and two bob a week!"

"That you, darling? Like me to take you somewhere for breakfast?"

"Act nonchalant — I think they've been tipped off."

"I want to report a theft."

"O.K. chum, this is a stick-up."

"Excuse me, young man, but I was here first."

"Please don't take that — I won it for unarmed combat in the Army."

"You cosh, and I'll swipe."

"We couldn't afford a divorce."

"Get a move on, Butch, or we'll miss 'Dixon of Dock Green'"

"Say you're not serious, mother if I knock over the bank you won't REALLY tell Santa?"

" . . . and when I closed my eyes,
expecting him to kiss me,
he beat it with my handbag."

" . . . silently the door opened and
into the room undulated a gorgeous
blonde wearing only a mask and
holding a Luger . . . "

"I HAVE taken the stocking off my head!"

"An 'andbag looks so effeminate!"

"And where do you think
YOU are going, Alfred?"

"I think we'd better break the gang up — that bank job only made us four-pound-ten each!"

"And two ice lollies."

"Be reasonable, officer — I was trying to lead her across the road by her handbag."

"Hallo, Mr. Briggs, I'm glad you're finally doing something about your overdraft!"

"Good, aren't they?"

"Your bath's ready, dear,"

"If you don't work hard in school how are you going to learn to write ransom notes?"

"I wish you'd stop putting your things in my wardrobe!"

"Just a minute — that barrel's FILTHY!"

"I was torn wiv doubt — wiv me delicate fingers should I be a brain surgeon or follow me Dad's trade?"

"What wuz the numbers on them false plates yer fitted?"

"First he puts 'im in a trance, then 'e tells 'im 'e's a tortoise!"

"Hello, officer — can I help you in your inquiries?"

"Police? Do we know any police?"

"Two hundred and forty-one (can't you see I'm busy?) Two hundred and forty-two."

"We're from the public library, sir!"

"On your way to work, take this to the 'All-night' Launderette."

"God bless Mummy, Daddy, Fido, and the burglar who's hiding behind the curtain!"

"I AM smiling!"

"Ain't yer got no pride in yer 'ome? Supposin' someone come round wiv a search-warrant?"

"I've been expecting you"

"You're not calling the police with your Mum on the floor and the house in this state?"

"Did you say you smelt bacon
frying last night, Myrtle?"

"Act nonchalant."

"Watch it — here comes the hostess!"

"I wish you'd take the top off your egg yourself, dear — this always makes me nervous!"

"But for that one little slip, you'd have passed your demolitions course."

"Had a wonderful day, darling: four confined to barracks and two detentions."

"I don't want to learn a trade or see the world — I just want to shoot people."

" . . . about two miles further on — you can't miss it, it's covered in camouflage!"

"Hullo — another cutback in defence spending?"

"I expect you'd like to sit with your mates . . . "

"This is the short-cut I told you about, Dave."

"Of course I still love you, Ethel
— R-I-G-H-T turn — D-I-Smiss!"

"I thought for one orrible moment
you were one of mine!"

"Good! You're beginning to get the
idea — I notice you tried
to fire back a couple of times!"

"Phew! I'll be dam' glad when my
walkie-talkie's mended!"

"Well, I suppose that's one way of
dealing with complaints, Sergeant. . . !"

"Let's go that way it's
much prettier!"

"And my old man was always saying, 'The Army will make a man of you'."

"Yes, it's the wife — I pinned it up so I won't feel so bad when I can't get any leave!"

"Gosh, Cedric, you seem to know absolutely EVERYBODY in the Army."

"Your task is to memorise and deliver a verbal message."

"Here are the volunteers you called for, sir."

"He's beginning to annoy me."

"It's all right, Sarge — I took my uniform off before I disgraced it."

"And when you retire I suppose you'll open a sweet little Army Surplus shop."

"Which is our side, I hope?"

"You manage to make a mess of everything — don't you Hargreaves?"

"There was nothing about THIS in the recruiting ads!"

"I'm going down to the cookhouse, would you like a bone?"

"MUST you park bang outside my office, Sergeant?"

"Watch it, mate — I made a bid for 500 vests, woollen, and found I'd signed on for 21 years."

"Good of the Sarge to give us the part of the chicken with the wishbone in, wasn't it?"

"Walkies again, chaps?"

"Well, don't stamp your feet so HARD, then!"

"I bought him at the
Army Surplus store!"

"Couldn't we leave it till
tomorrow? It's raining
cats and dogs!"

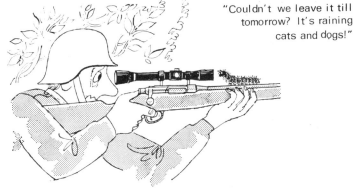

F

" . . . and I find I get tired and irritable after an hour in your waiting room!"

"I'm just taking the wife to the doctor — she doesn't seem well at all."

"The new doctor's one of those young, progressive fellows."

"Oh, well — that's show-business."

"I hate to say this — but exhale!"

"Shouldn't you be pushing your way to the front?"

"When you eat oysters, you're really supposed to spit out the pearls!"

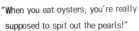

"Nurse! — Bees keep flying in and out!"

"Don't be too long with the stretcher, Fred — I think we've got another customer."

"It feels as though they're all fighting over me, doc!"

"You appreciate that it is hardly my job to ADMINISTER these nose drops?"

"Are you in a hurry for this?"

"Quick! He's swallowed a microphone."

"If you're looking for his chest,
it's slipped farther down the bed."

"I'm sorry, we can't accept any more of
your blood, your last pint bounced."

"Don't tell ME there's nothing wrong with me. I was in failing health
before you were born."

"Naturally I was frantic when you weren't on your usual train, then, three weeks ago, mother suggested I try the hospitals . . . "

"I'm a T.V. interviewer and . . . "

"He was here first!"

"Mother's very upset. She paid ten bob a pound for those mushrooms."

"Wouldn't you prefer to
read something, sir?"

"Miss Greenslade, will . . .
will you marry me?"

"I don't get it, nurse — he didn't
give ME any trouble taking his
medicine."

"First thing to do is loosen
the patients clothing."

"Hello? Pardon? Speak up!"

"Keep your husband quiet — and don't excite him!"

"Isn't it about time your doctor took you off that diet?"

"Sorry I lost my temper!"

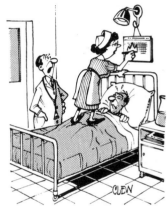

"Don't you think it would be easier to take the chart DOWN, Nurse?"

"Some smart Alec wants 'William the Corncurer!'"

"It's either lumbago. or your cufflinks are too heavy."

"Next please!"

"Now stroll outside. That'll cure your hiccups"

"You were lucky to get in, dear —
I understand there's a
big waiting list . . . "

"Could it be something she's
eaten, Doctor?"

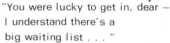

"Not doing too bad, for the
first day out of bed, is he?"

"This appendix . . . I think
the stitches are too tight."

"Off you go! — And if all my patients were as healthy as you I'd be out of work!"

"The first jab was for fibrositis.. The second was for being cheeky!"

"The telly isn't working and you think YOU'VE got troubles!"

"Better call me Mother — Father's a bit sensitive about the word 'Mummy'"

"Come back tomorrow — I've just had an urgent call!"

"Of COURSE you can hear a ticking noise — you left my wrist watch on!"

"We'll have a bed for you in a day or two!"

"Sorry to have got you out of the bath, doctor, but . . . "

"Now, my little man, there can't be anything very much wrong with you — put out your tongue!"

"Who's next?"

"I hear you've won the pools. What bad luck!"

"Aha! Too many parties!"

"No, doctor — it's my WIFE who can't stop hiccuping!"

"I'd like to find out what makes me tick — AND what makes me chime the hours and quarters, too."

"Dr. Miller, Dr. Fosdyke, Dr. Bruton and myself have come to the conclusion that you have a hang-over."

"He needs bucking up a little . . . such as you falling downstairs and breaking a leg."

"Now can anyone tell me what
Mrs. Smith did wrong?"

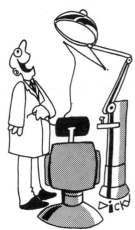

"Ha! Ha! They ALL do that when I
touch the nerve!"

"Your wife went home
yesterday — remember?"

"On your way out smile or the
others will think I hurt you!"

"You must give up smoking, drinking
and thinking about Mr. Wilson."

"Now, does that hurt?"

"Careful, Marjoribanks! — Do you realise the price of oxygen?"

"No, matron — in the lapel!"

"As far as I can make out from this prescription, you're suffering from potato blight!"

"Those were her very words, doctor — 'My feet are killing me'!"

"Don't worry about his loss of memory, doctor, it wasn't a very good one."

"Doctor! Complications have set in!"

"Yes, darling, the doctor's just confirmed it — you are about to become a husband!"

"Just keep taking the tablets and stop worrying about the side-effects!"

"You've got either a slipped disc or a large bra buckle."

"I should advise you to diet — but I just haven't got the nerve."

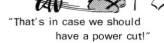

"Bit wider, Fred-"

"I'm busy now. Can you come back when you're better?"

"That's in case we should have a power cut!"

"Dip your headlight, doctor!"

"You don't often visit the doctor, do you?"

"My word, we ARE bitter about the Health Service aren't we!"

"Nonsense, Mr. Hill, we don't make mistakes in THIS hospital."

"Now here, gentlemen, we have a classic example of bingo throat . . . "

"The agony! — Mind if I go next?"

"If you must know, you fell off the trolley on the way to have your tonsils out."

"This one's a gardening mishap
— unfortunately it happened
on a roof-garden!"

"Lovely voice, my foot! He's
swallowed our transistor set!"

"These apples aren't as nice as the last lot I brought you."

"But why didn't you consult me as
soon as you realised it wasn't
athlete's foot, Mr. Johnson?"

"Don't join any walkouts
for the next two weeks."

"Just giving him his nose drops, doctor."

"In THIS hospital, nurse, we like to use more modern
methods of inducing sleep!"

"We get more calls from stranded motorists these days!"

"It's the mini-monk look!"

"I don't care what your name is — OUT!"

ANNUAL BAZAAR

"The church is okay — this is for the vicar!"

"I hate to rush you, Mrs. Higgins, but isn't it time you started scrubbing the floor?"

"It's not a bit like the book, is it?"

"Now, now, Mrs. Rigby-Smyth, your booking isn't till 3.15 . . . "

"Will Daniel be thrown to the lions or will International Rescue get to him first? Don't miss next week's episode!"

"Oh DO try to get there, Mrs. Plumley, it promises to be a real 'gas'!"

"Now, now, Vicar – stop pulling my leg!"

"Now I'd like you to meet the first of my Sunday Night People . . ."

"Frankincense fell at the last fence – pass it on."

"Now, Sister Margaret, try not to think about those ruffians who attacked you."

" . . . besides, they are off the danger list now."

"This is the church hall – the fancy-dress ball is farther along the street."

"Really, Mr. Marvo! – This is HIGHLY irregular!"

"The blighters are more resolute than I realised!"

"I've heard he was a train driver before he was ordained."

"Not fish, you silly woman!"

MANURE FOR SALE

"That's not what they've been calling me the last couple of nights, Vicar!"

"Now, listen — see if you know this one . . ."

"Marvellous meal, but we forgot to say grace."

"Johnson, you're yawning!"

Still — it keeps them from hanging around the streets."

"I've told you before . . . those are MY collars."

"I've heard his congregation is dwindling, but this is ridiculous!"

"What! You let the cat out last night!"

"Poor Polly's getting backache!"

"Ah! Here comes your big
chance now, Vicar."

"Good evening, vicar — this is an unexpected pleasure. I was just laying the table for my Fred's supper!"

"An actress called — said she had something to say to you."

"Out of the frying-pan into the friar!"

"Good evening! Tonight's epilogue will be given by a speaker from the opposition."

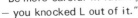

"Be more careful in future — you knocked L out of it."

"The Bishop wants to see me? What about?'

"Watch where yer goin', you big nit!"

"No thank you — The Vicar
needs it more than I do!"

"Go on to where the road forks
and take thou the straight
and narrow path."

"The Vicar's the one with the bow-tie!"

"Now, remember, if there's anything
you want — just go without it."

"That wasn't a bad show
for a tanner, was it?"

"And what name do you give this — er — bundle of washing for the Ajax Laundry, High Street?"

"Ah, Reverend, 'tis wunnerful the work God does, 'but 'e weren't makin' much of a job o' this garden 'til I give 'im a hand. . . ."

"I threw out a pile of your old sermons, dear!"

" . . . all the Disciples number 12, the Three Wise Men number 3, all the Commandments number 10 . . . "

"If you don't mind, sir — I'll conduct the ceremony in my own way!"

"Yer know, Bruvver Francis, this is a dead cush number compared wiv the 'Moor'."

"And there are others who come only to scoff . . . "

"Charles! Charles! The roof has fallen in!"

"You mean to say you've never HEARD of the Church Times?"

"Before we call the banns, here's a little book on Marriage Guidance and the address of a good optician."

"Don't worry, the little blighter's in here somewhere!"

"Another blinkin' letter from
St. Paul to the Corinthians!"

"Big service today, Forbes
Check organ pressure . . .
adjust lectern . . .
top-up font . . . "

" . . . As the actress said to the Bishop . . . "

"Hullo! Ron? You asked me to
phone if ever I found myself at
a loose end one evening."

"Sorry, Ben, but I just can't go
steady with you any longer —
I've got a crick in the neck!"

"Why, Ralph, I DO believe you're jealous!"

"I'm glad he's not just after my money!"

" 'COURSE I'll be home by midnight,
Mum — I'll have cleaned
John out long before then!"

" . . . and when I finally managed
to explain the gravity of the
export problem, I'm afraid your
daughter just fainted right away . . . "

"Sis! It's the one who can do
every bird imitation — except
migrate."

"Of course I'll have to get his
permission — he's my husband."

"All right, Mamma — I'm helping
Harold train to be a psychiatrist!"

"I'm looking for a boy with Dave's good looks, Mark's charm, Brian's manly physique an' Angela's hair."

"It's one of those holiday romances — her boy friend's in Majorca."

"OF COURSE there's no one else, Rodney — not on Mondays anyway!"

"I'm making headway with my bird. When she slapped my face last night she said, 'Sorry' "

"I hope dad likes you — he's very old fashioned!"

"Don't forget his lead!"

"Let's see, now — the meal was 16s. 10d. so your share is 8s. 5d. Bus fare 1s. 7d. and half of that is 9½d. . . . "

"And then he tried to tell me his record-player had run out of records."

"Do you mean to tell me Sylvia's already spent three hours getting ready to go out with THIS?"

"Sorry I'm late, but I find time rather drags when I meet you on time."

"Penelope's latest boyfriend's not much of a conversationalist, is he?"

" 'COURSE I don't expect your daughter to give up her career to marry me — ONE of us has to earn the money."

"I don't normally kiss on a first date, but seein' as it's also the last . . . "

"Careful! My father has the sofa bugged!"

"Suppose I should've jumped — I'm going to miss her."

"Must be one of those eternal triangles!"

"Well what boy's name do we have to avoid mentioning THIS week?"

"Isn't it romantic? — The magic of the night — your arms about me and the fresh clean rain beating into our faces."

"I know we're saving to get married, but do I HAVE to travel half fare on the buses?"

"I want my half crown back!"

"Linda Brown's flat is on the floor above — if you're still interested."

"Yes, it WAS nice of your father to let you have the car tonight, darling — when's he going to trust you with the ignition key?"

"Oh, no, sir — it was ME that screamed."

"I hope the fact that I'm a millionairess doesn't make you think any less of me, Rupert."

"We're so secretly engaged, Mum — that even Ron didn't know about it until now!"

"You never told me your brother had a smashing train set like this, Jean!"

"We've had a lovers' tiff about whose parents we're going to   live with!"

"I'm NOT trying to change the subject, dear — your slip really   is showing."

"You've been pulling your Christmas crackers a bit early, haven't you, Cedric?"

"He proposed to me and I turned him down, Dad!"

Careful, Justin! — If Mum hears me bell ringing, she'll be in like a shot!"

"Did you hear a faint cheer, and the chink of glasses?"

"Would your father be offended if I bought him a television set?"

"I KNEW she'd turn him down AND I'll bet she's scoffed all the coffee creams!"

"I'd better have an early night tonight, Doris, — I'm marrying Lucy tomorrow."

"Millicent, you aren't losing interest in me, are you?"

"Basil! I was just thinking about you!"

"A simple 'No'
would have been sufficient!"

"Show it to all the girls at the office
first, Mabel, then we'll flog
it and get married."

"Happy to have been of service
— see you usual time tonight,
Mavis."

"Mary, can you find room in your heart
for me?"

"And WHOSE is this long blond hair
I found on you shoulder, Helen?"

"Over here, Nigel!"

"I'd really love to go out with you John, but Bob would get so mad, he'd tell my husband."

"Sorry, dear — I didn't know you were so heavy."

"It don't worry ME if you've got scruples, darlin' — I've already 'ad 'em twice!"

"We're practically engaged — he's just waiting for his fiancee to return the ring!"

"Time to think WHAT over, Harold?"

"Believe me, baby — I've seen the light!"

"Next time, better think twice before you ask a fella like me in for coffee, Elsie!"

"Charlie! — Doreen's mother would like to see you!"

"If this squeeze isn't followed by a bout of severe restraint you'll get a kick in your marginal seat."

"You know, this place could convert nicely into two flats!"

"Don't take any notice — he's only showing off!"

"I'm not that sort of a girl!
I'm not that sort of a girl!"

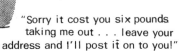

"Sorry it cost you six pounds
taking me out . . . leave your
address and I'll post it on to you!"

"Boy is he loaded! Last night
his wallet fell on my foot!"

"New condenser, replacing two faulty valves, adjusting
vertical hold, testing fuse . . . "

"Three cups of tea, finger marks on wallpaper, cigarette
burn in carpet, deep scratch . . . "

"On second thoughts, I don't
think I'll ask Dad to run us
over to Grandma's this afternoon."

"Then with the earpiece in you
can have the volume as loud as
you like without offending anybody."

"I have a request here, sent in by a listener . . ."

"I, the ill-informed idiot, enjoyed
the programme — what's the opinion
of the well-informed intellectual?"

"This set's a real bargain . . .
used to belong to a little old
lady with weak eyes . . ."

"A fine time to be called out,
halfway through the night
it's the Doctor again!"

"Tired? Listless? No energy?
What you need is . . . "

"A quantity of dynamite has
been reported missing from
Clinker Colliery. Will anyone . . . "

"I thought this play was
for television!"

"I have no statement to make
your wife and I are just good
friends."

"No, I don't remember snogging in the back row with you when
this film first came out in 1944 — I was in North Africa."

"Maybe it's funnier in colour."

"First time in forty years I've been
behind with me rental . . . "

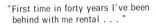

"Ours is one of the older sets."

"There's far too much sex on T.V.!"

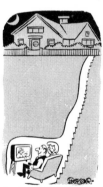

"Confidentially . . . "

"I'd still feel happier if we got a licence, Fred."

"I did it mending the T.V. set."

"Take it easy, luv — you've got nine rounds to go."

"The next programme comes via Early Bird and Eurovision links, especially for you."

"There goes the last one, Charlie — may as well play 'The Queen'."

"Don't they ever change the programme? It's been just like this ever since we bought the set."

"Albert! They distinctly asked you not to adjust the set."

"I think this tough interviewing business is getting out of hand."

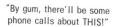

"By gum, there'll be some phone calls about THIS!"

"Is this a live programme?"

"For heaven's sake! — Here's my half of the licence money."

" Old it Fred! It's our request for our golden wedding anniversary!"

"We can get away with it on steam radio, but what happens if we get on T.V.?"

"It may be a gripping play, Harold, but please stop biting my fingernails!"

"Can I have it done on the National Health?"

"How do I know it will cause controversy? Because today's Monday."

"And now you have forty seconds to throw all these balloons into the air and catch them in the net fixed to this scooter!"

"Do you have visiting hours?"

"Normal lines of communication have broken down, but our man has got a message through . . ."

"The Prime Minister has assured us that there is no need for alarm."

"Feeling queasy? Try 'perk-pills' swallow two with a glass of water. Now watch what happens."

"Now just relax and forget that 30 million people are waiting to see you fall flat on your face!"

"Of course I've got a T.V. licence — I bought one when they first came out in 1946."

"Please don't adjust your sets I look like this!"

"You COULD have written to the B.B.C. about it!"

"I think you've got a winner here, with this 'Best of the weather forecasts' repeat!"

"Would you mind answering
a few questions, please?"

"Quick, dear, you're just in time
to see 'The Sky at Night'!"

"And now, a gale warning."

"Here's your off-the-cuff funny
comment at the end of the news."

"Trust your father to be waving a
filthy, dirty handkerchief."

"Cheek! They've shifted
their T.V. AGAIN!"

"I know one thing — she's getting too fat for a 21-inch screen."

"I still say we should have bought some furniture instead of a T.V. set!"

"Normal service will be resumed as soon as possible."

"Every time we switch on we get this effect!"

"Do I get anything if I answer the questions correctly?"

"Nip up the street and get a light bulb, Arthur — the television has broken down."

"This is the Recipes from Other Lands Programme."

" . . . and I tell you I've counted and counted and there are only 624 lines."

"Steady with the red, not so much yellow, easy on the green, a little more. . . ."

"It's a pity you haven't got an INFERIORITY complex. I'm rather good at those."

"You're not giving me enough time. Can't you put off your march on Moscow till next week?"

"Why do you want to see a psychiatrist? I like you just as you are, ~~dear~~ — kind, easy-going, stupid."

"He's fine until we get into the park, doctor."

"What d'you mean, 'Get on the couch'? — I AM a couch!"

"I'm told you've got an inferiority complex."

"Isn,t it amazing? That psychiatrist certainly cured our Myrtle's claustrophobia."

"See a psychiatrist? — I AM a psychiatrist!"

"How long have you had this fear of heights?"

"I don't MIND being a Hot-Dog, but the mustard ruins my clothes . . . "

"Yes, he IS perfectly normal, but shouldn't he be rebelling or turning into a hippie or something?"

"Now tell me, when you lose your temper, do you go to extremes?"

"Nothing much today, doctor — two Napoleons, one pink elephant, and a 'Nobody loves me'."

"This dream world you live in, Mr. Morton — how about taking me back there with you!"

"Now you say you have the feeling that everybody's staring at you."

"My feeling of failure started when I was a Boy Scout — a poor old lady I was helping across the road got run over."

"Henry — bath's ready!"

"What's all this then — the wife changed her bath night?"

"I'll be glad when our landlord mends the bath!"

"I see you've fixed the car."

'Mind giving this parcel to
the chap next door? . . .
He's having a bath!"

"That mirror, Henry? I got it at
a jumble sale — why?"

"Don't make such a fuss, dear,
you're not the first man to cut
himself shaving!"

"How much longer are you going to be in there!"

"Ethel, where did you buy this new linen basket?"

"An' when a politician gets elected, what does 'e do? I'll tell you. Nothing, mate, exactly NOTHING!"

"You owe me for ten pintas, two poundas, and three dozenas. I'll be glad if you'd pay off parta if not alla!"

"Yer said I could work stripped to the waist didn't yer?"

"I do quite a trade with the office-staff."

"Can't wait for a lovely cuppa when we've finished, eh, Mike?"

"My mother warned me never to accept suites from strangers!"

"Leaving early, Bletherwick?"

"Actually, I never wanted to be a factory hand — I wanted to work on a farm!"

"If he could tell the time, I reckon he'd be a clock-watcher."

"We always walk across the street like this . . . it's a great joke!"

"He's very street proud!"

"Amazing what Lil will do for a few extra bob!"

"If the men don't get satisfaction,
they're liable to turn ugly!"

"Nice bit of lagging—
what a pity it's scaffolding."

"Brr! — Nice to get outside!"

"I've found the electrical, fault,
my dears — it's a blown fuse!"

"I distinctly said NO mustard! . . . Now
get back there and tell him . . ."

"The days don't drag so since I had the radio fitted."

"And now a really fabulous group direct from Dublin—
The Murphy Brothers."

"I tell you blokes it'sh no use
— the lasht one's gone."

"You bin workin' for me all this time and now
I find it's only a second class honours
degree you've got."

"Let's take another look at the plans, shall we?"

"Sorry, Benson, I'm
putting you on short time."

"Get lost!"

"There's another ten minutes to knocking-off time, Johnson."

"Don't worry, sir, — your wife can't make up her mind what colour she wants the ceiling!"

"Very nice indeed, Hornsby The only snag is this happens to be a glove factory!"

"I see, sir — oyster lustre ceiling and emerald mist walls. Fred, fetch a tin of white and a tin of green."

"All that fuss because it's the wrong way up."

"Blimey! Have you seen what's round the corner, Bert?"

"Ballcock and valve please"

" . . . and this is the staff canteen."

"There's no doubt about it — she was the best canteen manageress we ever had."

"With assets of £5½ million, you'd think this lot could afford a step-ladder."

"Maybe we should have left a hole down the centre!"

"The job's a bit dull, but we get our exciting moments. Yesterday I held a straight flush at poker."

"She loves me!"

"Any butter, eggs, cream
or tinned fruit, madam?"

"This has got to stop, Martha, have
you seen his overtime rates?"

"When you've been fitted with your
overalls, report to me."

"I promise you this'll be the last time, Jackson — the wife comes home tomorrow."

"We've got four aways, six at home and two have gone for a perm!"

"Would you mind checking your catalogue? You've dusted my husband twice!"

"They're our two chief test-pilots."

"After thirty years' service we're presenting you with an engraved watch. Now, what's your name?"

"Typical! Lying right where I wanted to clean . . . "

"He started a new job today '— as a steeplejack."

"Vandals!"

"When were you thinking of trying to get me to come, luv?"

"Oi! There's a little room down here full of lolly!"

"It's not a REAL strike — they just like to keep in practice."

"Good to get away from it all at the end of the day, isn't it?"

"Somehow, Mills, I feel you're unsuited to this work."

"I'd love to come in, but I've left my ladder and bucket round the other side."

"I told you to use the SMALL roller!"

"I'm truly sorry you've been doing competitions for twenty-five years without a win, sir, but . . . . "

"I said you could start ON the night shift. . . . !"

"Harry's been very good to my brother — he's set him up in a second-hand clothes business."

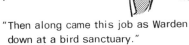

"Then along came this job as Warden down at a bird sanctuary."

"I see old Fred's having one of his 'Rejected by Society' moods again!"

"If at first I don't succeed — I quit."

"All the time we've been talking, those men have been leaning on their shovels."

"Never mind, Mick, the barrow's sure to turn up one day."

"For Pete's sake, Bert! . . . We'll find your teeth when we get to the wagon!"

"It's nice to know Hubert's in a steady job."

"Keep it up, Jackson, we've almost sold out of our cameras and binoculars."

"All I know is, it does something to within a thousandth of an inch."

"Testing department here . . . "

"Can't you wait until tomorrow to
sweep that up? — This is
your day off!"

"These tea-breaks seem to be
getting out of hand!"

"There's nothing for you.
I repeat — NOTHING!"

"Town Hall? Over there."

" . . . and quit usin' it fer yer
smalls, 'iggins!"

"Ah! I see where you went wrong — you want 23, Laurel AVENUE!"

"It's a walk-out . . ."

"Shan't be long — going to check my pools."

"In appreciation of your fifty years' service, Maclean, we'd like to overhaul that watch we gave you twenty-five years ago."

'I'll never understand how you won that 'Beat the Clock' jackpot."

"If you don't like sago pudding, go and tell the shop-steward!"

" . . . so I decided to settle here where I can get on with my writing."

"Notice how that new bloke is sucking up to the Foreman?"

"If you don't watch out, the blokes'll begin to notice there's 'somefing between you and that canteen bit."

"I just got the sack!"

"It's his half-day."

"How did YOU think we made the holes in colanders, then?"

"That's odd, Your Royal Highness
— I felt sure he'd stop."

then the wife suggested
entering this petrol competition
and, well, here we are!"

"I gave strict orders that the
Mayor's Parade was for local
shopkeepers only!"

"It's just what I wanted!"

"Hm! No underfelt!"

"No no, James — the poisoned
soup is for His Excellency!"

"Actually, His Excellency seems
quite friendly, I think it's
the interpreter who doesn't like us."

" 'Let's go into exile' you said,
in a few weeks they'll be
begging us to come back', you said . . . "

"You may take my word for it; sir — this is NOT the room in which the last round of the darts tournament is being played . . . "

"Well, don't just sit there who's got a bob?"

"I wonder what they'll be trying on to get into Wembley today, Fred,"

"That's funny! I've never seen him standing before!"

"He should have been on a horse but they ran out of money!"

"Wake up that man at the back there!"

"Hector —you need a haircut."

"Fred! Are you SURE Her Royal Highness has gone?"

"And now that I'm going — I'll tell you what I REALLY think about your wretched little country!"

"A guinea for your thoughts!"

"Pardon me, Minister, but when you sign a treaty you don't put 'All the best' before your name!"

"When you've finished commanding the bath water to go out, your supper's ready. . . ."

"Honestly, you make me wish I'd never married a commoner. . . ."

" . . . and quit slipping out before the end of the National Anthem."

"All right! All right! I'll declare war then — anything for a bit of peace."

"We had a very frank and friendly meeting!"

"I distinctly said $6\frac{5}{8}$!"

"It's a frank, personal story I've written about my ex-valet."

"I'm beginning to **regret** we game HIM the freedom of the city."

"I thought you said you were reviewing troops today. . . ."

"Ah, well — that's progress I suppose!"

"Ah, General, I see you're wearing that medal I sent you for Christmas!"

"Sometimes I wish you'd never started tracing back your silly ancestors."

" . . . I suppose you wouldn't happen to have a tanner on you for the collection. . . ."

"Now, what's a nice girl like you doing in a place like this?"

"Going over a cliff wasn't bad enough, oh, no — YOU have to land on a submarine."

"Don't forget your tool kit, sir!"

"Could I please have a word with someone about after-sales service?"

"Hey, Bert, we've got a stowaway."

"But I hardly scratched the paintwork."

"The lid on my toolbox is jammed."

"Did you know that all the rain we've
had has made the garage shrink?"

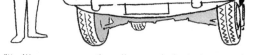

"You'll never guess — the policeman who booked me was the
living image of Sean Connery."

"Right — now forward a little."

"There she goes . . . driving him to drink again!"

"It's your own damn fault . . .
I was taught to drive by your
school!"

"Money can't buy happiness, but at least
it would buy automatic transmission!"

'You and your 'Special Offer Honey-Boy After-shave Lotion' . . . !"

"Let's make up our minds who is driving this car — you
or your mother!"

"Trust YOU not to notice that I vacuumed the inside of the car for you, today!"

"No, that's reverse!"

"Sister Veronica! — Remember your vows of humility . . . !"

"Dad! . . . Mum's devalued our car again."

"Shteady, dear! . . . Mind that Posht! . . . Watch out for . . . "

"Thank God you stopped him officer, he's been cutting me up all along the road."

"Well, I think YOUR optician ought to have HIS eyes tested!"

"My word — but for your very prompt action in slamming on the brakes — we might have run over that little dicky bird!"

"I'm only firing on 143 cylinders."

"Act nonchalant."

"Mind you, our County Council isn't a patch on Hobshire!"

"I suppose you COULD say it's rather heavy on petrol, sir. . . . "

"Well, sir, one DOES get teething troubles with a new car."

" . . . Well, it's stopped!"

"Are you SURE your boss doesn't mind us using it for weekend trips to the seaside?"

"Yours says, 'Good day for showing initiative, creative ability and sheer brute strength!"

"Three dozen dark grey addressed to my wife . . . Christmas gift wrapped of course!"

"I don't think the little chain at the back's working . . ."

"Unfortunately my husband considers that the loss of his no claims bonus constitutes mental cruelty AND incompatibility."

"My husband is sweating on a 40 per cent, no-claim bonus next month!"

"Well — it COULD mean 'No Entry'!"

"WHEN are you going to get these ruddy lights fixed?"

"But Freda! — It's got to come off sometime!"

"You only have to sit in the first car on the first stand and bang goes my No-Claim Bonus!"

"While we're waiting for the police, would you care for a little refreshment?"

"Silly boy — it means 'Beware of man having trouble with his umbrella'!"

"I don't know what came over me — I suddenly had this overwhelming desire to see all the lights on together!"

"Faster, Henry! The guarantee expires in three minutes!"

"Sure it's a long starting handle, the engine's at the back."

"I'm as car-proud as anybody, but when it comes to polishing the UNDERSEAL. . . !"

"I just HAD to see you again, Harold!"

"Always remember to signal before you move away, it stops accidents."

"Hello . . . hello . . . what's my little woman been up to today?"

"Traffic lights ahead, dear . . . better get landing permission!"

"Kindly stand clear, sir, while I release the bonnet."

"You'd better fetch the petrol — I'll stay here and see if I can get her going."

"The outside, you nit!"

"Not very good at spelling, are you?"

"It's making a sort of guggly, fizzy noise — like when you pour champagne into your bath. . . ."

"Everything I do lately seems to annoy you."

"I'd have passed you if you hadn't run into that chicken."

"The windscreen washers are back-firing!"

"Well, we had a garage at the other house!"

"I was very careful, George — I drove to town and back with the handbrake on."

"I'm looking for something with a bigger boot."

"Phew! That was a bit tight – I didn't think we were going to make it."

ROY NIXON

KLUTCH'S SCHOOL OF MOTORING

"Right hand down a bit, Mr Sibthorpe!"

STAFFORDSHIRE

"D'yer have to make it so obvious that this is our first car?"

I

"There it goes again — I knew I heard something knocking!"

"Now shall we try getting into the car again, Miss Faversham?"

"I want to report an accident!"

"I wonder why no one else is using this Motorway."

"And I suppose if I don't get it back
by twelve, it turns into a pumpkin."

"It's in good nick, except
for these odd items. . . .'

"No, darling, not 'Water in the
motor' 'Motor in the water!'."

"Perhaps a member will show up."

"I made it from an old silencer!"

"It says 'Road liable to subsidence!'"

"Left hand down a bit!"

"Charlie! — Slow DOWN!"

"Harold's a long time finding out where the nearest garage is, mother."

"Hello! — who's this come to see us in a battered old wreck of a car?"

"I think we're getting over-staffed again!"

"Anything else? Water? Oil? Wicks trimmed?"

"I was against mine learning to drive, too."

"When I had a bike, I used to test 'em in a bucket of water!"

"How do I know you're not Danny la Rue?"

"It costs a fortune in petrol, but you ought to see them trying to tow it away!"

"Have you a book on changing a car wheel?"

"You can wake up now Henson — the car you were repairing has gone!"

"Hopkins! I'm the one who does the selling here!"

"Your battery has passed on."

"Give us a kiss, then!"

"Oh dear, I do hope it's not an even date."

"I'm afraid it didn't do so well in the road test!"

"Try it now!"

"How's that for brakes?"

"Terrific, Miss Pugh — that's the left turn solved! Now let's sort out the timing."

"I got nicked last night — no flippin' rear lights."

"A.A. breakdown?"

"Well, I can't see them!"

"You know — the Insurance Company will never believe this."

"See you five miles down the road!"

"Congratulations, sir, you've won this week's 'Pick-a-Car Contest'."

"Before we discuss taking you on as an instructor here, would you kindly GET OFF MY FOOT?"

"Midships, Commander — midships!"

"Never again do I go to a firemen's dance!"

"I hear they simply WRECKED a train on the way."

"When we come out of the reverse turn, in future take one pace to the LEFT."

"And now meet our judges
for the military two-step,"

"None of your tricky steps,
now, Freddy . . .

"Mr. Fenner — there is a buffet
at the far end of the room!"

"Sorry, but I appear to be
booked for the next dance."

"I've never known such a
crowded dressing-room!"

"O.K., you got a deal —
three wishes it is, then!"

"Oh yes, the glass slipper fitted
all right, but when I kissed
him he turned into a frog."

"If I give you another kiss would
you turn back into a handsome frog?"

"That's YOUR story — how do I
know you're really a prince?"

"She makes lovely porridge."

"It's all relative, innit? From one point of view, I'm just a very big dwarf."

"Hold it, she's one of ours."

". . . the handsome prince turned into a juicy frog, and they had him for dinner and lived happily ever after."

"We're warning you, Guv — either that compost heap goes or we do!"

"Now that's what I call a MAN!"

"We'll be along about eight o'clock, not seven — Desmond always takes such a time dressing."

"Oh no! Not my lovely big borrowing cup!"

"Remember asking what I did around the house all day? Well, today I DIDN'T!"

"Dinner's ready, darling, bought with my very first housekeeping money."

"Yes, my Arnold retired last week. Proper gentleman of leisure he is now!"

"If you ask me, it's like livin' in a bloomin' mosque."

"There's nothing wrong — I always take a ten-minute break every two years."

"Looks like it's true that her husband's left her!"

"Why don't you play with your kids like other fathers?"

"Myrtle, you really should strip the spare bed more often."

"This washable wallpaper is all very well, but it's such a job getting it off the wall!"

"I'll tell you why Mummy's hands are always so soft and beautiful. Because she always lumbers me with the washing up, that's why."

"We did the dishes for you mum. Dad washed, Peter wiped, and I picked up the pieces."

"There's a new liquid dish-washer in the cupboard, George — just one squeeze!"

"Quick, hide! My husband's coming!"

"There was a time, Mildred, when I looked forward to your retiring from show-business."

"I've just got to do the washing, ironing, dust the place, change the beds . . . I'll be with you in about ten minutes!"

"You're not going out until you've helped your Dad with the washing-up."

"I wonder if that's the 'Hot-Line'"

"You're going to look a right nit if it don't snow."

" . . . and you call yourself a plumber!"

"And I tell you Sir Walter Raleigh used his OWN coat."

"Brilliant forecasting, Woppleton, the Met Office is proud of you!"

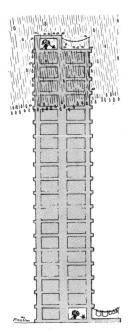

"Oi, Mary! Rain on the way!"

"Looks like rain, doesn't it, dear?"

"So THAT was the noise I heard last night!"

"Exactly what they forecast on T V."

"First, a word about last night's hurricane."

"You read the weather forecast fine, Smith — it's just that they didn't like the adjectives you used!"

"I'm sick of getting drenched!"

"Ar! You should have had 'em lagged mate!"

" 'Morning, Mabel — quite a wind
last night, wasn't it . . . ?"

"Hello . . . A.A?"

"If I don't get a rise soon I'm
flippin' well going to have . . ."
my corn removed!"

". . . Tomorrow will be bright with sunny
periods — weather permitting."

"So that leaves YOU top of the class."

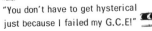

"You don't have to get hysterical just because I failed my G.C.E!"

"Playtime's over, Miss Hollister."

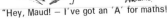

"Hey, Maud! — I've got an 'A' for maths!"

"And the science teacher said to tell you that a good stiff dose of castor oil ought to do the trick!"

"He's teacher's pet — she keeps him at the back of the class in a cage!"

"That's me teacher, dad — punch 'er in the nose like you said!"

"This one we're training as a lawyer — looks like the others are going to need him!"

"This 'apple for the teacher'
business doesn't apply at
university, Harmsworth."

"It sounds all right in theory,
but does it actually work?"

"They've been striking me for years!"

" . . . and this is Simpkins,
our geography master!"

"It would need only a quick
rinse to brain-wash him!"

"Robin's told me so much about you, Mr. Cartwright — I can't think where he picks up such language!"

"What's this I hear about you teaching the boys to play Russian Roulette with the starting pistol?"

"Miss Larkin! Playtime is for the CHILDREN!"

"I flogged two boys this morning — got seven-and-six each for them"

"Right! — Now empty the other pocket"

"You know all these emergent countries? Well, that composes their national anthems."

"Here's a laugh! There's a guy out there who says he can make people invisible!"

"Are you sure it'll work, Orville?"

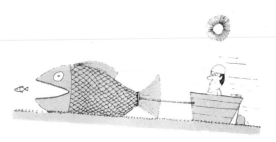

"I know it's very clever, dear, but I'd still rather have an eye-level grill!"

"That's so he can't snore."

"Would you kindly ask the next genius to step in?"

"Hello, Frank. What's new, then?"

"Am I right for London Airport, officer?"

"What d'you mean dad's done it at last — done what?"

"That's funny — I can't turn it off, now."

"Pass the sauce, please."

"So THAT'S what made the milkman's horse bolt!"

"You danced divinely last night, but shouldn't you have had a partner?"

"This tea tastes like strychnine!"

"Have you changed much over the years, dear?"

"Blimey! Once married, some women couldn't care less what they look like at breakfast!"

"Did I forget to boil your egg again, dear?"

"Tomorrow's our first anniversary — if I can just stick it out."

"I see the dentist's sent you a white feather."

"Oh, Charles, how sweet and where's the flippin' paper?"

"Helen! You have all day
to read the paper!"

"Krunchie-Flakes are GO . . . "

"It's lovely, darling, but at home
we usually had something a little
simpler for breakfast."

"DO try not to drop crumbs
on the carpet."

K

"The feeling is mutual, I can assure you!"

"Guess what, mother? We're
expecting another bundle of joy!"

"I'll fix up a baby-sitter and we'll go right out and celebrate!"

"They announced it over the loudspeaker, so I rushed here at the final whistle!"

"My! What a lovely pram!"

"We've really enjoyed this little get-together, Effie. You must have another baby soon!"

"It's a tadpole!"

"It's laundry, stupid!"

"Tell me quick — how many?"

"A boy at last! It'll be a great help when he gets a paper round."

"Well, Fred's wife had TRIPLETS."

"I'd better take two — we've just had twins!"

"Everything's fine — and the gravy stains don't show up all that much on the ceiling."

"Gracious, Eileen, so THAT'S why you rushed out before the end of the movie!"

"Then, after nappy-rash and windy-pops, will come your greatest trial — toothypegs . . . "

"But, Mary, I distinctly told you I wanted a BOY."

"Darling, you mean we'll soon be hearing the chatter of tiny teeth?"

"How I'd like to get married and get away from all this."

"There must be a stack of them behind that hill — one drops
behind there every night."

"I like them myself — mind you, I
wouldn't let my daughter marry one."

"Smashing new secretary — look at her biceps!"

"How many times do I have to tell you not to be cruel to helpless
creatures?"

"Yoo, hoo, dear! What's for supper?"

"Don't panic! His brain is only as big as a hen's egg."

"Go home, Spot."

"My grandfather told me that before the nuclear war he had to get down on his knees and propose before he could get one of these!"

"But, Ug — supposing a brontosaurus!"

"VERY clever! — Now invent the wheel!"

"I distinctly said I wanted an omelette for lunch!"

"What is a pretty girl like you doing in a stuffy little cave like this?"

"He's company for me."

"Well, at least Daddy's left us well provided for."

" . . . these cold mornings it's
a devil to get started . . ."

"Brontosaurus? Roast for two
moons in volcano at regulo 90°."

"Reckon Og is stocking up for the winter!"

"Just think of it, Madam, no dirty, dusty corners to clean out!"

"I'm looking for a garret to starve in."

"Cosy little kitchen, isn't it?"

"To give you an idea of this neighbourhood's status, sir, that's an abandoned car over there."

"Must it have a moat?"

"I thought there was a catch in it somewhere — you don't see many bungalows at that price!"

"Hw. Did yu Knw. I ws. an Este. Agt?"

"We'd like something near a school."

"I'll take it — send it to this address!"

" . . . with a basement!"

"This area has the worst housing shortage in the country!"

"Ask him about the foundations, Fred."

"It looked a bit bigger in the photograph, didn't it?"

"I know your ad. said 'half-timbered', but this isn't quite what we imagined."

"A room with a bath, please."

"I'm checking on reports that you're sub-letting your council house, Mrs. Moxon."

"I told you they were very strict here about guests being prompt for meals!"

"That's my husband — he's an art student like yourself."

"Of course she's my wife.
Think I'd bring her to a dump
like this if she wasn't?"

"You're in Room 176 — here's your
key and mousetrap!"

"Heh! Heh! Smith, eh?"

"And could you inform us as to the
whereabouts of the local flesh-pots?"

PATON.

"Carry my wife's luggage?
Heavens, is SHE here?"

"Dammit! — You're overloading
again, Fudwell!"

"I suppose Rover IS an unusual
name, really. You see, my father
wanted a dog!"

"I'd like a room with a bath, please!"

"He's certainly putting that roadwork to good use!"

"This is your final warning, at least three of those punches were below the belt."

"One thing about Gleason, folks — he never gives up trying."

"No wonder he's angry — he cleared ALL the fences and I didn't clear any!"

"Now there's something you don't see every Saturday!"

"There are rumours this fight's been fixed, lads
— not that I believe 'em . . . "

"I see Smithers is playing with his boss!"

"Rafferty! Come out of there and fight!"

"Ah! They're getting a little arm-weary."

"Nobody ever gives ME a kiss."

"Can you come back next week?"

"C'mon — take it, man!"

"But Mr. Frisby — you lost!"

"I think you'd better go, darling,
Fred's been sent off."

"Now we know why Bert 'iggins' pigeon 'as bin champion
for so long!"

"To think my wife is snug at
home decorating the landing."

"Go on — kiss it better!"

"You can't give up now . . . you're nearly out of Dover Harbour!"

"Missed it again!"

"Oh no!"

"Don't look now, but isn't that our new goalkeeper?"

"That horse has never won a photo-finish yet!"

"You've won!"

"How about that for an unbiased opinion!"

"Hold it there, lads — this one's for a ball-spotting competition!"

ST ANSELMS CRICKET CLUB

OWN F.C. SUPPORTERS' CLUB

"I see they've reported back for training!"

"I'll say this for him . . . he's a good loser . . . "

"When do you reckon it will be our turn to stage the World Cup?"

"Excuse me, is this Karate night?"

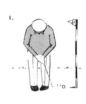

1.

2.

"How much farther to Dover, Bert? These stilts are killing me."

3

4.

5.

6.

"I thought that was an unusually long tunnel!"

"Hey, Ali! You're praying in the wrong direction!"

"Are you quite SURE you're a qualified guide?"

"Guess what, dear!"

"Blimey! You're right! It isn't Dover, it's Southend!"

"It doesn't look as though he's
going to try to beat the count."

"Look — I'm sorry I said
that about your mother . . . "

"That's funny — you're the third 'arold Wilson I've booked this afternoon."

"Can't I forget about strategy and just fight for my life?"

"You're in luck! I've managed to fix you up with a return fight!"

"I'll wear my teeth this round — he's biting."

"It ain't against the law to hit him back, yer know."

"They mark their men well, don't they?"

"Did nobody ever tell you?
You're a dirty rotten, poor loser
you are!"

"Let's see what it
says about lost balls!"

"Don't you dare get blood
on those clean shorts."

"A little too much height on that one, Mrs. Leach."

"Don't count your winnings yet, Fred — there may be an objection to this one."

"He likes to rest his horse right up to the moment the race starts."

"Oh! Oh! It seems to be a rather nasty cut!"

"We haven't decided yet, but we'll probably appeal against Jack's death sentence."

"I meant to tell you, this is a rather tough course!"

"What do you mean you're glad that's all over? — That was only the weigh-in."

"I know — you think I'm NERVOUS, don't you?"

"Hurry up! The batsmen are still running!"

"This warm-up fight you say you should have had — that was it."

"Put me DOWN!"

"Is that you, George? How's the home-made boat?"

"Do yer best, Ginge — 'e could be a Spurs talent scout, yer know."

"I think you'd better master the punch-ball before I put you in the ring with a real opponent!"

"Both boys are in the ring now — the champ looking sun-tanned, fit and glowing with health, the challenger, a little paler but still in peak condition . . . !"

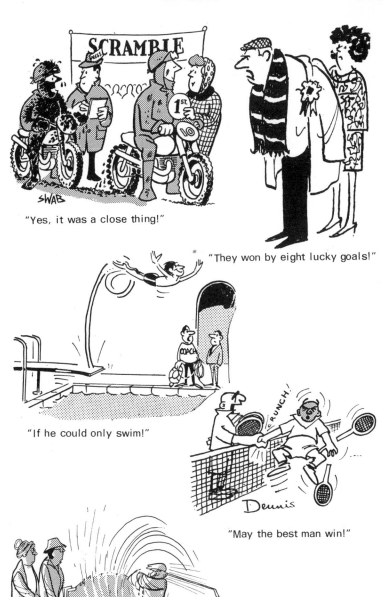

"Yes, it was a close thing!"

"They won by eight lucky goals!"

"If he could only swim!"

"May the best man win!"

"Hilda and I are going off to tea now, dear — don't go away . . . "

"Charlie's trained hard all year
to get in for nothing!"

"Excuse me — are you sure
you've fought bulls before?"

"Put me ashore at once, Sidney Brown!"

" . . . and in this corner,
a moment ago . . . "

"This is almost as bad as the drive down here!"

"Me an' the missus will be down for coffee on Wednesday, then."

"Fore!"

WRESTLING TONIGHT

" . . . and in this corner at thirty stone two pounds . . . "

"Pity he's such a poor in-fighter."

"Cynthia— you're not trying!"

"Do you think they ought to have a saliva test?"

"O.K. Pringle — sound the 'Retreat'."

"Pssst! Take a dive in the fifteenth."

"The champ's taken his defeat rather badly!"

"Well, it's a good fight,
but it's not a GREAT fight."

"There's been some
misunderstanding, I fear."

"You made me look
a right Charley out there!"

"Congratulations, sir! You've
just hit a ball in one!"

"You were lucky that time, dear —
you nearly lost it down that hole!"

L

"For Heaven's sake,
Sam, play another ball."

"Congratulations on winning! Now I expect you're looking forward to the second leg."

"Fat chance I've got of getting to Dover if I have to keep going back to Calais for petrol."

"That reminds me — we're out of breakfast food!"

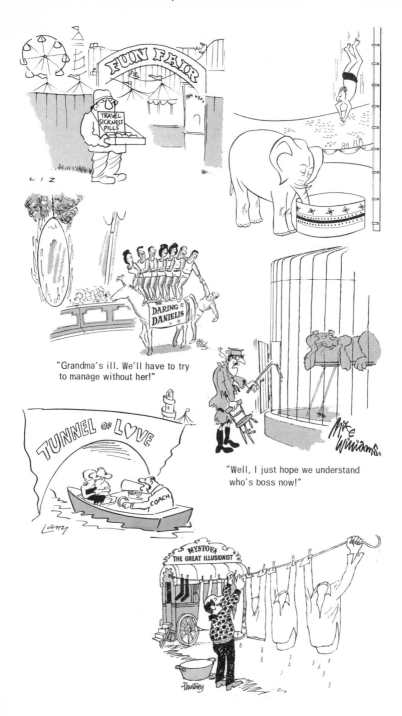

"Grandma's ill. We'll have to try to manage without her!"

"Well, I just hope we understand who's boss now!"

"COURSE it's blurred — 'e was a short-sighted butler."

"It's a good act, but I have to keep buying new dogs!"

"He always takes hiccups terribly badly."

"Control to Oscar Charlie One — get back in formation."

"I don't know what's come over him — he never used to have a temper like this!"

"Whoever ate the cleaner gets no supper."

"The job is only temporary — the other chap might eventually come down."

"There's two old maids operating a pirate ship in there!"

"I wish you'd lay off that plum-pudding at lunch, Charlie!"

"I suppose we shouldn't have, really — they're terribly fattening."

"Been here so long I forget what I really look like."

"You're going to have chicken pox."

"This journey I'm going on—do I find a place to park?"

" . . . then, after the terrible accident, you'll go down with mumps and then, just as you're getting better . . . "

CRYSTAL GAZERS ANNUAL CONFERENCE

" . . . and just where have YOU been all night?"

"Now our worthy secretary will read the minutes of NEXT year's meeting!"

"Of COURSE you can see me pushing a pram — I've been a nurse-maid for five years!"

"I don't like it . . , she just closed her account."

"Yes, I can make it tomorrow, dear, but YOU can't — you're going to slip a disc . . ."

"You'll meet a lovely blonde — but wait — she's just gone into a hairdresser's."

"Begorrah! It was yerself told me you'd like to read me fate!"

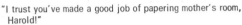

"I trust you've made a good job of papering mother's room, Harold!"

"Would you mind holding this nail for me, dear? — I always hit my thumb."

"I've made you a stick, dear — to mix the paints with."

"You know, Ralph, sometimes I wish you weren't QUITE so handy around the house!"

"Haven't they got a home to go to?"

"Ethel!"

"How's it going?"

"Ah, well, made a start — now for a pint . . . "

"Blimey, I don't know how that Michelangelo bloke did it!"

"See? Daddy KNOWS when he's doing wrong!"

"Got any Do-it-Yourself jobs, Missus?"

"It doesn't seem very labour-saving to me."

"On the other hand, she's a lousy cook."

"How much did you pay for this paintbrush, Ethel?"

"He makes the most beautiful, hand-finished firewood.'

"Does running the tap help?''

"Now, I want you to imagine I'm
a little girl five years old . . . "

"I may be wrong, but I get the impression
she's trying to avoid giving
us a Christmas box."

"Don't I need to show you one or more
of your products and then answer
a simple question before you
give me anything?"

"I hate the thought of Fred being stuck in the chimney all winter
Mother — whatever shall I do with that ton of coal?"

"Don't ask Dad to help — it will only
remind him of his lost licence!"

"Let's face it, J.B. . . . . Our idea of an
office party may not be everybody's!"

"We thought this model would be more in
keeping with the spirit of Christmas."

"How many more wretched threepenny bits are there in this
Christmas pudding?"

"I didn't get no 'at in me cracker!"

"No thanks! I bought him a hedge-trimmer LAST year — and there was nothing left of the Christmas tree by Boxing Day!"

"Is it REALLY necessary for our cat to send one to Wilson's cat?"

"What's he advertising, Dad?"

"I hear everybody's having a grouse this year."

"If it will make you happier we'll add the word Xmas!"

"All together, now — 'Noel, Noel, Noel . . . '"

"I'd like to order a 19-year-old blonde about 36-23-36."

"I'd like Jolly Roger to win the 8.15 please."

"Watch it! The Guvnor's car is just coming round the corner."

"Congratulations! . . . At last a hair-spray that works in a Force Nine gale!"

"9, 10, 11 . . . seems to be one bug, missing, Professor!"

"Can I borrow a cup of type 'B' virus?"

"Is this the way to the brain drain?"

"It wants to know what happened to the dishy blonde who used to bring it flowers."

"And this is me and the wife at Blackpool!"

"Well, Billy's dad works for the Ministry of Defence."

" . . . but suppose United don't want to pay thirty-thousand . . . "

"Hi fellers — I'm back!"

"Helluva draught coming from somewhere, Charles."

"10-9-8-7- . . . "

"You know the rules, Barker — no strangers in the lab."

"Thorndyck won't be in today, sir — touch of bubonic plague."

"What a breakthrough, Hawkins — now we've got someone to clean up!"

"Do stop trying to destroy the world with that, Fenton — it's only the gas meter."

"Can't you ask it what's gone wrong?"

"It says 'To err is human'!"

"The second cup is NEVER as good as the first."

"Meet Professor Brownski,
the electronics expert."

"Mrs. Bagley, you've been at my
cocktail cabinet again."

"I've never met such a
flippin' knowall!"

"But what are you going to
DO with the world when
you've taken it over?"

"Shall I be mother?"

" . . . Don't forget to change the
Budgie's water, we owe the milkman 10s.,
your clean underwear is in the bottom drawer . . . "

"You never take me away
for a holiday any more, Gaston."

"Off out again with the boys? . . .
I wonder sometimes what I get
out of this marriage!"

"So they've made you captain of
the darts team! What do I do now
— curtsy?"

"Well I like that! A strange man
follows me, and you say 'Probably
some nut'!"

"I'll say this for their marriage
— the physical side's not dead."

"Good heavens, Edward . . .
your hair's going grey!"

"You might at least have put a
clean towel on to answer the door
Alfred!"

"You're drenched, dear.
Go and stand in the sink."

" . . . and another thing — when are
you going to fix this pram-handle?"

"Putting his foot down? — Rubbish!
She hit him over the head
with something!"

"Wipe your feet!"

"That's right — make the ashtray untidy!"

"Thought so! — You didn't wipe your feet!"

"You never buy ME any ants's eggs, do you?"

"I want something feminine and dainty, yet capable of a good, sharp kick."

"Captain speaking — abandon ship!"

"Nothing like a good lie-in on a Sunday, is there?"

"Until the food runs out you have no reason to fear me, Miss Estwitch."

"Dear Mum, I hope you will excuse writing . . . "

"That 'Permission to grow a beard, sir?' joke is no longer funny, Murphy."

"We mustn't look on this as just another holiday romance, Miss Newson, promise me you'll write."

"Full ahead — both!"

'The post's late this morning."

"I'd call it a day, sir —
if you don't want cramp."

"I suppose this is what you
call shark-infested waters!"

"Oh, it's you. I thought you'd
gone down with your ship."

"I have a confession to make —
the ship wasn't really sinking!"

"A fine way for my Prime Minister to carry on, I MUST say!"

"Don't just stand there, Johnson — BLOW!"

"Why can't you do the washing on Tuesday?"

"Let's see now — 3½ years at 6d. per half-hour . . ."

"I told you we should have gone First Class!"

"Women and
children first . . . "

Right, lads! Get the lifeboats out!"

"I'm organising a ship's concert . . . "

"Uncle Fred was a ticket clerk for over thirty years,"

"You've hit a bull, Gaffer "

"Throw us back, you fools, we're top secret!"

"Very good, sir, 480 pounds — including your wife."

"Liar!"

"I think the boot put up a better fight than the tyre!"

"That's right! Go rushing off somewhere the minute your lunch is ready."

"Never mind the goldfish, fix that tap washer."

"Catch anything . . . ?"

"Moose, Canada 1953 . . .
Tiger, India 1957 . . .
Ethel, Liverpool 1938 . . . "

"Awkward things to shoot,
kangaroos — aren't they?"

"You see, we could never
afford to go abroad . . . "

"The sailors say it
means good luck . . . "

"Don't you think we're using
a bit too much groundbait?"

"Cor! — Friday again already?"

"I said, 'Throw it back!'"

"Sorry, ol' chap — you shouldn't have jumped in my line of fire."

"Go on, say it! — Only ONE?"

"You certainly know how to train gun-dogs!"

"Anything else, sir? Confetti?
Lucky horseshoes?"

"CUT!"

"Sorry I'm late, you folks."

"Oh no — YOU couldn't be content being an internationally famous film star, YOU had to make a movie."

"He told me there's no truth in the rumour that they're just good friends."

"They certainly set an example to some people during the National Anthem!"

"Before we were married, you used
to hold doors open for me!"

"I tell ya, this is gonna be
the biggest thing since
Lassie!"

"That was great — try it once more
then we'll start shooting!"

" . . . so, she was born in a trunk, eh?
— After THAT performance she should be
found dead in one . . . "

"Let's face it, Smith, as a
projectionist you're a flop!"

"It comes out all right in
the end — he shoots her."

"Take us in, mister?"

"One single at 2/9d."

"What's it like?"

"Hang on a sec, Jim — you get a
simply wonderful stereo effect from
the middle of these one-and-nines."

"It's all yours, Shirl!"

FAMOUS FILM STAR WEDS IN SECRET

FULL STORY AND PICTURES INSIDE

"O.K. Forbes — you were hired as my stand-in for the CHARIOT RACE!"

PLAZA

"The coat's fine, sir, but this weather I'd like trousers, too."

"Cut!"

"Who the heck wrote this screenplay, anyway?"

"You shouldn't be out so soon after your accident!"

"Plenty of seats Sir — they're queueing for the back row."

"He's been making too many war films. Last week he had an actor shot for insubordination!"

"PLEASE, Ethel, it's only the flavour-of-the-month advert!"

"By the way, I ordered a new fur coat this morning."

"Go on, honey, marry me — just this once!"

"Put more life into it, you're supposed to be dead!"

"I've had a good look round, dear — see if your shoes are among this lot!"

"But how was I to know it was the children's performance?"

"I don't understand it — why didn't he marry both of them?"

"By the sound of it, Ron, that must have been a very funny film!"

"Bit stingy with the chips, aren't they?"

"George, do you happen to have a Henry the Eighth penny on you?"

"Let's wait here. These two look like a couple of fast eaters."

"Have you been riding in
the plate-lift again?"

"This place must be under new management
— it used to be such a nice little
teashop back in 1948."

"If you don't cough up
the protection money
— we'll wreck the joint."

"That'll be one and tuppence, and next time get yerself a tray."

"A pot of tea for two, please!"

"There's ham and fag-ash, salmon and fag-ash, or egg and fag-ash."

"Yes, it has a certain joie de vivre, but I think the Darjeeling '65 had a better bouquet."

"We run a skeleton service after 8 p.m."

"You've got the choice of two madrigals, nalf a dozen sonnets or a minuet!"

SELF – SERVICE

TODAY'S SPECIAL — SAUSAGE AND CHIPS.

"Say when!"

MUM'S REAL HOME COOKING

"Come on, now! Eat up your spinach!"

"No, you can't have a rise . . .
and stop borrowing the gipsy!"

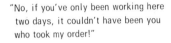

"No, if you've only been working here
two days, it couldn't have been you
who took my order!"

"I assure you, sir, it's not the
same steak you sent back.
HE'S eating that!"

"May I borrow this a minute? — My
wife wants to see what today's
special looks like."

"The service here is so terrible,
it's a good place to rest."

"Before you order, Miss Peabody, I must tell you all about a MOST interesting
intestinal blockage I operated on this morning."

"Here comes the head waiter, Phoebe — you know, I think you SHOULD have worn a tie!"

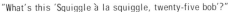

"What's this 'Squiggle à la squiggle, twenty-five bob'?"

"On second thought, I'll have the rabbit!"

"I'll try one of those karate chops!"

"Girl? . . . What girl?"

"A fly in your soup, sir? I'll phone the Rescue Squad at once."

"What do you mean, the Manager's gone to lunch?"

"I wonder what spoilt this broth . . . ?"

"You don't have to tip me, but we do like to keep a friendly atmosphere between staff and customers."

"I don't like your attitude — are you insinuating I was trying to sneak out without paying?"

"You don't have red wine with FISH!"

"Thank you waiter"

"I'd rather go somewhere else, Charley."

"Can't you read?"

"Is this the only way you can tip him, Maurice?"

"I'll be with you in a moment, sir!"

"Do yer do a businessman's lunch, cock?"

"Sorry! I lost my glasses and thought it said 'Girls'."

"No, you AREN'T expected to sit there till you starve — we close in ten minutes!"

"One thing about this place, at least the food's good."

"When in an Indian restaurant, try ordering in English!"

"Why don't you just TELL them that the chicken's cold?"

"I'd like a look at that bill!"

"Whoever called this job WAITING?"

"He didn't flinch — you sure you put everything on his bill?"

"Waiter — the fly in my soup was cold . . . "

"I won't tell you again — it's 'May I take your order, sir?' Not 'Hands up for stew'!"

"And the chef sends you HIS compliments, sir."

"The smile is 6d. extra."

"The management regrets that fourteen luncheon vouchers will NOT be acceptable, sir . . . !"

"Get a move on, Chef — that bloke on table six is getting impatient!"

"In a place like this you'd think they'd have electricity."

"The time, sir? — Sorry but this is not my table."

"To be on the safe side, Henri, scratch whatever that gentleman had, off the menu."

"Well, you shouldn't have spoken to the gipsy violinist like that!"

"Glad you fell for that hard luck story, Guv. I'm 'is scriptwriter!"

"Readin' was never my strong point!"

"One day, Bert, I'll make the big time. I can see it now 'Wife and TEN children to support'."

"I'm thinking of settling down!"

"I'm minding it for a friend!"

"Could you spare enough for two cups of coffee? I got married last Tuesday."

" 'Bye dear, have a nice day, see you tonight!"

"Expensive? Kindly remember where you are, madam!"

"Just browsing, thank you."

"You know, sometimes I wonder if it's all worth it."

"Come back home, son — all is forgiven."

"Now that we've established that you believe in free speech, my good sir — may I use your phone?"

"Thanks all the same, old man, but I don't need it; I'm an eccentric millionaire TOO!"

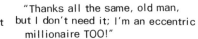

"Have you any tramp steamer cruises, mate?"

"Before I decide, what's the floor show like?"

"So I says to him, 'O.K., loudmouth, let's see you take my companies over'!"

"Coffee, rubbish — what you need is a good booze-up."

"You must FORCE yourself, you poor fellow!"

"You must be joking!"

"I'm arresting you for desertion in 1947 . . . "

"GENUINE hard-luck case — this morning he was a fully clothed match-seller."

"It's simply LOVELY, Arnold —
but Daddy hasn't even given his
consent, yet."

"Spare a bob
for a couple of blades, lady?"

"Who'd think that, a few short
months ago, he was the World's
leading authority on brown ale!"

"You don't know where your next
meal's coming from? You're lucky!"

"After all, I'm leaving the field
clear for blokes like you to
make your pile!"

"Ever thought of selling your story to the newspapers?"

"My wife found out I was working overtime — she thought I was meeting another woman."

ST. MARKS ORGAN FUND PLEASE GIVE GENERO

"I'm not an expectant father, lady — I'm collecting fag ends."

"Bad news, darling — I've lost the Bert's Pie Stall account!"

"And enter our surprise guest for the evening
— with her inimitable patter — MISSUS BLOGGS!"

"Rover's certainly taken a fancy to your after-shave lotion!"

"Don't be silly, of course you're not keeping us up."

"They DID say Thursday, didn't they?"

"We sat at home all evening wondering
who we should visit, and you won . . . "

" . . . I'll say this for Edna — I can bring the boys home for supper at any
hour and she'll always rustle up something . . . "

"Rumour has it that's where he keeps the booze."

"I shouldn't be talking to you like this
. . . you've probably got troubles
of your own."

"This pie is delicious, Mrs. Bundy.
Tell me, how do you manage
to make your pastry so thin?"

"Don't worry about the wife — she's
wonderful at handling these little
emergencies!"

"Ignore her, Fred — she'll do anything to stop me watching the late night
movie."

"Ashtray, Mr. Loomis?"

"Darling! How TRENDY! —
Wall-to-wall floorboards!"

"I didn't keep butting in. I was
merely trying to say goodnight."

"We don't have television — Alfred
believes it kills the art of self-
entertainment."

"Did you come on your motor-bike?"

"I sometimes get the
impression you're ashamed of
me when we have visitors."

ARTHUR

"Oh! Not MORE pictures of
your baby, Mrs. Grimble . . . ?"

"Did you notice the dust
on his mantelpiece?"

"You're lucky having a handy
husband. Bert can't even
put a new washer on the tap."

"Let's have some kids of our own,
then invite THEM over."

"I didn't mind their holiday films, but not those commercials
for her ruddy dressmaking he stuck in!"

"Do excuse my husband not speaking
— I'm afraid he's rather shy."

"Thanks for a lovely party, darling
— and we won't have to worry about
being stopped for a breathalyser
test, will we?"

"Does it occur to you, dear, that
Mr. Perkins might care for another light
ale?"

"Sorry we're late — the
traffic was terrible!"

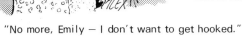

"No more, Emily — I don't want to get hooked."

"Forgive us if we can't stay long
— Keith has had a rather tiring day."

"That's the last time THEY come
to supper — not a perishing word
about our central heating!"

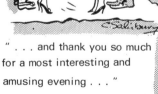

"... and thank you so much
for a most interesting and
amusing evening ..."

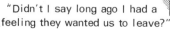

"Didn't I say long ago I had a
feeling they wanted us to leave?"

"I'd have insisted on you folks having
a drink, but there's a big wasp
trapped in our wine cabinet."

"It's Vietnam, Cedric!"

"He's far too old for her. They say he was at Aldermaston in '63."

"Sorry! . . . I've lost the way!"

"But, Dad — YOU'RE always painting slogans around the place."

"Had any luck?"

"More trouble-makers!"

"Way out, man!"

"This is the worst organised spontaneous demonstration, I've ever been in."

"He used to be with M.I.5"

" . . . then Betty and I got married, and the twins were born, so I just HAD to go commercial!"

"The film, Angela! — Throw out the FILM!"

"I'm beginning to think we'll NEVER find this Explorers' Club!"

"Of course it's wet. I've only just finished it!"

"Platform ticket, please."

"What a monstrous bone, Farqharson! I wonder what it belonged to?"

" . . . Professor! — This is no time to be diagnosing an inflamed epiglottis . . . !"

"Anyway — I proved that witch-doctors can't turn men into midgets!"

"At least you might have got us round the flippin' corner!"

"One thing you've learned, friend, they weren't kidding."

"Simple! — My son nicks 'em from a shirt factory."

"At that price you should be wearing one over your face."

"It's a little bit of psychology they taught me on the firm's salesmanship course."

"If that's another of those darn salesmen . . ."

"As I always say, Madam, there are a lot worse things you can have than great big flat feet."

"Do you mind? — I'm busy."

"Since I became my own boss I'm not taking orders from anybody, dammit!"

"O.K. sir! So much for the soft sell, then!"

"Ah! Do I see a man, lonely and ill at ease at cocktail parties through limitations on interesting conversational subjects . . . ?"

"The little darling wants to go flysies."

"Just as I thought! Selling your soul to the devil as soon as my back is turned!"

"I'm fed up with being the lesser of two evils!"

"This is my brother Joe. Good lad, really — but he just couldn't lay off the women!"

"You strike a hard bargain, Madam, but I agree — Eternal Youth AND a million stamps!"

"Every time Khrushchev makes a speech I have to get millions and millions of beds ready."

"It's just gone twelve o'clock, my lady!"

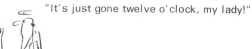

"He left his body for medical research!"

" — and three weeks ago I was conducting a hundred-and-fifty-piece orchestra!"

"Mr. Smith! — You've been eating sticky toffee again."

"Do you ever wish that you could develop a severe attack of chilblains?"

"Been sent down then, have you, lad?"

"What's the score?"

"Boy! I'll be glad to get between the sheets tonight!"

"Off again in a few moments, folks!"

"That new route with the low bridge was a piece of cake."

"For goodness sake! What's gone wrong THIS time?"

"No, mine's not among that lot – I'll try St. Pancras!"

"Well, you asked us to pass Father down the bus!"

"Dare you to slam the gate and ask him for his season!"

"About 7lb 2oz., with fair hair and blue eyes."

"Please yourself — either pay up or let go!"

"I'm afraid there's little hope of them turning up after a month."

"Now look, sir — wouldn't it be easier just to buy another ticket!"

" . . . in his late forties, balding, about five foot seven, weighs nine stone and drinks too much — on second thoughts, I won't bother."

"Hi, beautiful — get lost!"

"Sorry I'm late . . . but you know what the trains are like!"

"I was wondering when you'd turn up!"

"Come on, dear — open your mouth, the inspector wants to look at our ticket!"

"I left a case of Stilton here three weeks ago . . . "

"They don't run very often."

"Excuse me — you're standing in my place."

"Sorry I'm late — had a breakdown at Darlington."

"Mind turning round, young man? I've read this side."

"Is THAT all right, smart Alec? — Now 'oppit!"

"I understand they're bigger than a London bus — and more frequent."

"No, NO! — It was a WOODEN one!"

"Well! 'Ave yer got a
ticket or 'aven't yer?"

"I know it says 'No Smoking'. It
also says 'Wear Slimmo Corsets'!"

"Straight on for ninety
miles, then turn left."

"Room for one more inside."

"No, you want the 26B — it goes
right past the Black Lagoon."

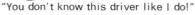

"You don't know this driver like I do!"

"That's mine — I can smell my cheese sandwiches!"

"Did you hear that? — It sounded just like a gunshot."

"I have NOT turned communist, Saxby — I've just come off the Underground."

"Well, there definitely is NOT a body in it, You should've locked it — people'll pinch anything these days, y'know . . ."

"The jam roll going off early in your canteen is no excuse for doing seventy!"

"Trust them to come today with our front room all of a mess with the paperhanging . . . "

"I've phoned the Air Ministry, and they say there's a perfectly logical explanation . . . "

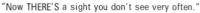

"Now THERE'S a sight you don't see very often."

"Hey, Brian! Come and take a butcher's at what we've been worshippin' for the past million years."

" . . . and stop throwing dirty saucers out of the window!"

"YOUR job, Fenton, is to determine whether the surface is hard or soft."

"Crikey! — I wouldn't like to meet THAT in a lonely spot on a dark night!"

"Greetings, earthman!"

"O.K. – the next time around, bop it one!"

"What do you call that thing?"

"If Paleface think him going to
take THIS land from red man,
him got another think coming!"

"They're all alike y'know – the minute they land, straight round to
the National Assistance."

"Why is it always me that
has to empty the ash-tray?"

"Well, is there an association we
can contact that DOES believe in us?"

"He's pretty nimble for someone
who's lost a leg."

"Hard luck, Arsenal's playing
away, but if you fancy a look at
Fulham . . . "

"Oh, no! Not earth again for our holidays."

"Something tells me it's one of those days."

"Hi! Grimley! — The chief particularly
said leave the local girls alone!"

"Last year I went to Bude."

"Couldn't see a thing, eh? Next
time you're sent to Mars pack
your razor, Tovarich!"

"Cor! Freddie — have you seen your stars today?"

"It must be ten past three. There goes your daddy!"

"Next week, I'll sell you another casket of earth treasure!"

"I'll let my Bobby out to play with you WHEN he's done his homework!"

"Thank goodness! I'd almost given up hope!"

"How was it — apart from the meteorites?"

"Well, I just hope it IS an advertising stunt!"

"Isn't it marvellous to think that your husband is up there making history . . . ?"

"This is the life! Better than just drifting aimlessly around!"

"Nice to get out in the sun again, isn't it?"

"You're turning that plant into a hypochondriac!"

"This one is strictly for the enthusiast!"

"You MUST cut the lawn — what will the people on the ground floor think?"

"Hello! Sent you into the exercise yard too, has she?"

"Fred gets very depressed with gardening."

"You sure old Blowhard's gone to lunch? Let's have a look at the mushrooms!"

"Now twist round!"

"Working up a thirst for opening time?"

"You mean you've been up all night prising open their tiny jaws and stuffing it down their throats?"

"They call it The Sunday Morning Derby — losers buy the winner a pint."

"I still can't decide — try to look more like a tree."

"By golly, you were right, Fred — it isn't celery!"

"Do you mind doing your sunbathing somewhere else till I've finished this bean trench?"

"Throw yer garden open to the public at 'arf-a-crown a head, then you'll be able to afford yer OWN lawn-mower!"

"Don't pretend you can't hear your wife calling you, Charlie I can hear your knees knocking!"

"Well, have you ever thought of filling it with petrol?"

"I said I'm sorry — what more do you want?"

"Ah, well — who's going to race who in making a nice cuppa, this bright and sunny morning?"

"Hi, gorgeous — I could lie here all day looking at your beautiful face, but I suppose you have to go and make a cup of tea, you have to . . . "

"Did you remember to lock up?"

"While you're up, Fred, get me a glass of water."

"Talk to me, Ethel — I can't sleep."

"I wish you'd remember to press your trousers BEFORE I get into bed."

"That is what I call a spring mattress!"

"Herbert . . . is that you creeping downstairs for a sandwich?"

"Bert — I'm sure I can hear somebody downstairs!"

"Henry — it really IS about time you fitted a longer flex to the electric blanket!"

"Are you SURE you've switched off the electric blanket, Edna?"

"Huh! So an alarm clock isn't good enough, now you've won the Pools!"

"Wipe that grin off your face — I do believe you've burgled mother again!"

"Paralysed, indeed! Next time you come home drunk be more careful how you put your pyjamas on!"

"Don't you think you should
close that window?"

"It looked better in the advert,
but it was a nice try, Ada."

"One-third of the world starving,
and YOU'RE feeding your SKIN!"

"Listen! It's three hours
since we saw that film!"

"There you go again — breathing!"

"I've only got a COLD, Gladys!"

"Hey, Dad! When I put my finger in
the corner of your eye
it goes click!"

"For the last time, darling
— either HE goes or I do!"

"Get a good night's rest, dear
. . . there's something I want
to tell you in the morning."

"Dreamt I was on the M.1., darling."

"You DO need a holiday, Albert.
During the night you sold me four
brushes and a broom."

o

"I've just had a funny dream, Ethel!"

"After you've shut the window, darling, pop down and see who's ringing the door bell."

"I thought you were going to start some sort of new beauty treatment tonight, Sylvie."

"Mum! I just whacked a burglar! Where's Dad?"

"Nice try, Walter . . . "

"Been downstairs all night, Pa — helping a man to pack for his holidays!"

"This getting up and going to work every morning, breaks up my whole day."

" . . . and this is where the Duchess and I sleep."

"You rang, sir?"

"I keep meaning to phone the taxidermist about that!"

"So ends my first day as children's nursemaid at the Grange. Something tells me this is not a happy house."

"Dammit! If the A.A won't come, phone the R.A.C.!"

"That's a rotten lie! We were just good friends!"

"Do you mind if I smoke?"

"Oh, you ARE lucky! — I wish I had some poor relations!"

"Would you care to wait in the library, sir? It's down the road next to the Town Hall."

" . . . and a dash of soda on the starboard whisker, James!"

"Will that be all, sir?"

"We're worried about Cynthia. So far no Lord Right has turned up."

" 'Er Grace says 'Belt up'!"

"Arnold, do you realise your soup is getting cold?"

"I've just had an argument with the gardener, dear!"

"I DID speak to him, dearest,
but he didn't answer."

"I always said they were a couple
of big-heads!"

"It's the neighbours again, complaining
about the noise from our radio."

"I think we had better let him
have his lawn mower back!"

"And by just giving that knob half a turn to the right, we can blast the
neighbours out of bed!"

"Really, Mr. Mason! What if your wife were to come out?"

" . . . and the wife should be
well enough to collect
the gossip herself
again next week."

"What I like about you, Fred, is
you're such a good listener."

"Maud's getting suspicious of me keeping
running up here to complain about
the noise."

"My husband never
buys me anything!"

"They don't feel inclined to keep
their party quiet, but they're
dedicating the next song to us."

"I understand our new neighbours are in some kind of show business!"

"No, we don't bother with T.V. Actually my husband is thinking of buying a cinema."

"Proceeding along High Street, I observed Maggie with a male, whom I knew not to be her husband . . . "

" . . . and another thing I don't like about her — by the way, is that the sun setting or rising . . . ?"

"Bob does that now and then — he doesn't believe in getting too friendly."

"Miss Lushbody — I'm from the flat below, aren't you going to come down to complain?"

"To whom it may concern . . . first we have a nineteen inch T.V. set, followed by a studio couch, two occasional tables and . . . "

"The wife isn't too well, so if you've any bits of bad news to cheer her up . . . "

"Did I miss much while I was at the Doctor's this morning?"

"They're the biggest social climbers in town."

"Oh, that's our next door neighbour. Funny, she usually only comes to borrow a cup of sugar."

"Mrs. Patterson said we'd be one of the nicest couples in town, if it wasn't for you."

"I'm frae downstairs — would ye mind turning your radio up? We can hardly hear it."

"Go on, get out — you're fired!"

"Good morning — can I help you?"

"I'll need more proof of your experience as a steeplejack, than that!"

"I'm sorry, we've no vacancy for a freelance Peeping Tom just at the moment."

"I'm not happy with my present employers!"

"I suppose when I get a job you'll forget me and these stolen moments together . . . "

"What else can you do besides reign?"

"Actually we get very few demands for a vandal."

"No, it doesn't look as though I've got a vacancy for a mercenery at the moment."

"I tell you it isn't EVERY man who's replaced by an electronic brain!"

"We're from weights and measures!"

"Luck is with you. You will win your next heavyweight fight."

"Help! Help! I am plisoner in honoulable Japanese tape lecorder flactoly!"

"The first of your thirty-six easy payments is now due."

"Obviously the pot hasn't been warmed."

"That dam' thing forgot the one for the pot again . . . "

"It's not going to be much of an office party this year."

"It might be laryngitis, there's a lot of it about!"

"Four pounds off this week — you DARLING!"

"Now to find a SIX stone weakling to kick sand over."

"You are easily taken in by silly gimmicks or nonsense you read on cards."

"You're 7 stone 8 pounds and you'll come in third."

"And this is how you set it for hedge trimming."

"They say it's a great tonic but I haven't the strength to unscrew the lid."

"Idiot! You're supposed to kick sand in HIS face, not HERS!"

"Certainly I want you to drive me over to my Keep Fit classes. You surely don't expect me to WALK!"

"AFTER you've done the body-building course, you fool!"

"Mulligan! — I told you to keep this door CLOSED!"

"No, no — you still haven't got it right Mrs. Hawkins."

"It's about time you gave up these evening press-ups!"

"Exercises be damned, Madge — I've got cramp!"

"How did you guess we'd attended yogi classes before?"

"You ALWAYS wander off when dinner's ready!"

"And I tell you I bought the last one."

"Beat it, will ya? . . . Go fly round and round like the others."

"You might have waited till I got a drink before you put your feet in."

"The agent was right about there being no competition."

"We'll have to stop seeing each other . . . my wife's getting wise to what happened to the Foreign Legion."

"Taxi!"

"Some people have no shame, forever cadging lifts."

"If you're thinking of asking her for the next dance — forget it!"

"We've got to stop meeting like this, girls — my wives are getting suspicious."

"We must organise a proper sandpit for them."

"Loitering, eh?"

"I wish she'd hurry up — our house is on fire."

"Go jump in the lake."

"Get back to the fire!"

"Will you shut up about the smell of woodsmoke on an autumn evening?"

"Who's out of date? — We've got the fastest horse in the county."

"All right, where's the fire?"

"Put her back, Johnson — wrong address!"

"Quick! Run for it! The house is on fire!"

"Thank goodness you've come home — your supper's, burning again!"

"Please wait until you've heard their story
before you get cross, Mr. Dingwell."

"Ought to be locked up — he's
deliberately trying to cause
unemployment,"

"In the circumstances, I'll give
you the last 200 cubic feet
at the cheap rate."

"Not that one, Furnaby
— that's our decoy!"

"This should baffle them."

"But I only stopped to tell you
I'd passed my driving test, Dad."

"Just look at this, chaps — another STUPID article about
the Civil Service being overstaffed and underworked!"

"That's nothing — you should see
what they do if you pick
the flowers."

"You're too keen, Crombie
— wait until they stop."

"I'm booking you!"

"Would you mind leaving us, Miss Perkins? I'm afraid he still owes us four and eightpence."

"A tax-man's life is hard, the pay's poor, the hours are long but, oh, that delicious feeling of power!"

"Shouldn't we TELL him he's been transferred to another department?"

" . . . and no drowning either!"

"His widow says he can't pay his tax because he's dead — there's a feeble excuse for you!"

"Those tyres are bald, Mrs. Phigley!
Get them changed immediately."

"I've come to switch yer gas off!"

"I think this new Librarian
is going too far!"

"Just don't expect any tea tonight
— that's all!"

"Well it hadn't bloomin' well expired when I got in this blasted queue!"

"You haven't put whether you're Mr., Mrs: or Miss, Mr. Toogood."

"I'm not sure about him. Did you notice his three-second delay when they called 'Tea up'?"

"It was nice of him to sign it."

"It's Bert with another load of bigamists."

"I didn't let MY wife talk to me like that..."

"Hey, Fingers — I've 'ad
a real smashin' dream!"

"...and this is one of me
at Pentonville last year."

"He's going down a bit deep for
planting tulip bulbs, isn't he?"

"You'll never get away with it."

"Oh, and the new lodger sends his regards!"

"I've a feeling somebody grassed!"

"In all the years I've stood out there, this is the first time that anyone has ever asked me in!"

"Betty and Fred got married last week, and you're invited to their fiftieth wedding anniversary!"

"Goodbye, mother — and lay
off the booze. . . ."

"Did you thank them for having you,
Tommy dear?"

"Let me know when it's
stopped raining, Officer."

P & D. KEATING.

"I'd like a look at the menu,
please, my good man."

"My goodness — this is quite a view
you fellers have up here."

"I think of my family on fine days
like this — the kids playing
truant and the missus nicking
fruit down the market."

"Say 'Bread and Water. . . .' "

"Oh, dear, now I've started hearing voices. . . ."

"Can't these little jobs round the house wait till I get out?"

"I'm the Jones all the others were trying to keep up with."

"Dear Joan, the drill arrived okay; now smuggle in the air-compressor."

"I blame the telly — what was YOUR excuse?"

"And stop addressing my letters 'Number 3529 Esq.'!"

"Alf — I want my freedom."

"Sure, an' oi'll have the flamin' lot of yer in solitary together!"

P

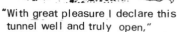

"With great pleasure I declare this tunnel well and truly open,"

"Frankly, Marjorie, I couldn't care less about Fido coming out of quarantine today!"

"Why the heck can't YOU do their ruddy homework?"

"It's NOT an escape rope — it's my winter-weight string vest."

"Fred, you mad, passionate fool — you DO still love me!"

"My compliments to the baker and the Water Board."

"I also believe in having separate holidays, but not seventeen years running!"

"There's been a breakout at the Scrubs."

"Well, if it ain't Perry Mason!"

"Well, if you're planning on escape make it after dinner, I've only got enough food in the house for one!"

"Now when I was young, we'd count ourselves lucky if we could break out once a year!"

"I'm sure I left the cooker on."

"I'm warning you, Boggs! If you don't give yourself up NOW you'll miss bedtime cocoa!"

"I fell out of bed. . . ."

"I've lost track of time, but I know I'm due out on..."

"... and to commemorate your 25 years here, we've decided to present you with the Governor's watch."

"The Joneses have planned three escape bids, but you just sit there!"

"Sid never SETTLED here ... he was never really one of US"

"Mind you, I'm not as good at it as you."

"But Mom, it was dark in that alley — how could I tell it was you I was mugging?"

"We've got a man from 'White Wiz' washing powder coming here tomorrow to do a commercial. . . ."

"Escaped prisoner in a grey uniform? No I ain't seen him."

"Nobody can touch Big Louie when it comes to organising a break!"

"Business is so bad lately our bouncer has to throw people in."

"I can always tell when Norman has had enough . . . he'll go stiff as a board."

"It's not a fit night for a dog to be out — "

"I try to take an interest in anything Ben likes."

"I don't think he's a busker — I think he's plastered!"

"I don't suppose you feel like coming out to some stuffy pub to hear a load of boring conversation by a shower of boozy men . . . ?"

"When I'm sloshed, switch me on to the cheaper brands."

"Why don't you give up, Henry? You'll never beat the Breathalyser."

"Sixpences, sixpences — haven't we got a whisky bottle with WHISKY in it?"

"Bingo!"

"Is this the same gay, carefree husband who set out to row the Atlantic last night?"

"A desperately sad case — his wife left him, but his mother-in-law stayed."

"Do you know you were drunk last night?"

"A Merry Christmas to you, too! — But this happens to be December 29th!"

"I thought we might celebrate my safe return from the pub. . . ."

"He was so close I could feel his hot breath on my face. Fortunately, he could feel mine, too!"

"You're always starting fights in bars and getting us thrown out."

"I t'row myshelf on the mershy of the court!"

"Like to hear a taped playback of your triumphant homecoming last night?"

"Taken you two a long time to post a letter — what delayed you?"

"Thanks for bringing me home, Fred, only that doesn't happen to be ME!"

"Albert! Have you been DRINKING?"

"Psst! Bushter — know a good lawyer?"

"Well, hello! — Arthur's always talking about you Mrs. Wilson . . ."

"Free love? Disgusting! The least you can do is to buy'em a drink!"

"I've had an absolutely frightful day, looking for a job for mother."

"I've never heard of whisky going flat if it's left in the bottle!"

"Is that right you got stopped the other night?"

"What makes you think I'm drunk, Muriel?"

"Stella! Tell me I'm not just four pints of bitter and twenty fags a night to you!"

"Sad case! He won the Pools the same week as his boss."

"Have a word with him, Albert. He hasn't stopped complaining about my Bloody Marys all evening!"

"Ah, well — time I was off to the pub . . . "

"How about Rachmaninoff's Prelude in C Sharp Minor?"

"Psst, Fred! Thanks for the 'Hullo, George, long time no see! when we came in."

OFF LICENCE

"You all 'eard what that chap said. Gimme some brandy."

"Ever wondered why our marriage is a success, Liz? It's 'cos we've got the same interests."

"Shtop honking the horn, idiot — you'll wake my wife!"

"I've just won the treble chance, mon — drinks all roond!"

"Aw, come on, you've seen me sober before."

"You're going to miss that cold when it goes, Charlie."

"From what I can gather, you and your wife seem to be drifting apart."

" . . . all right, then — you're a bat — but when you wake up in the morning, heaven help your belfry! . . . "

"I've no idea who she is — but she comes in for 5 pints of mild every night!"

"Well, did you have your 'Man-to-Man' chat?"

"I wish you'd tell your wife to stop bringing your dinner in here, Fred."

"I'm not your wife, and it's not visiting day at the prison!"

" 'ullo! Looks like another row over the scoring!"

"Don't be silly, Edith — if I told you where I'd been you'd murder me!"

"My wife told me to stop drinking or she'll leave me. Gimme a large Scotch."

"Enjoy your half-pint and don't go getting into any punch-ups."

"TIS I! — Your lonely vigil is ended!"

"That's Mr. Dobson, my boss."

"I was going to say you'd got him out late — I didn't know you were taking the empties back!"

"Coming in at this time of night — don't you know it's nearly October?"

"Well, how are things with you then, Taff?"

"Of course you haven't got DT's — she really looks that way."

"An Englishman's home is his castle, offisher — I happened to fall into the moat."

"He's only shouting 'Last Orders', then it's 'Hurry along please', then it's 'Time gents' then we go in the back room."

"Oy! Don't go starting a new chapter — we're going in a minute!"

"It could have been the happiest marriage in show business if she hadn't gone off with the registrar."

"Well, you told me not to sit around all day drinking tea. . . ."

"I mush shay, you have beautiful big feet."

"Do you realise this is the 7,500th night you celebrated your demob?"

"Mummy will tell you a story soon. Daddy has one to tell her first."

" I think you deliberately let life overwhelm you!"

"Go on, Maud — tell me what kind of idiot I was last night!"

"Stop shouting, Alice — people will think you've been drinking."

"Greta, I do wish you told me about coffee mornings sooner!"

"I can't stop long, Fred — I only came out for a bucket of coal!"

"The period of severe restraint didn't seem to bother you till it was your turn to buy a round!"

"Your trouble is you hate to see me looking happy."

"It'sh no good tryin' to talk me out of it — I'm goin' to jump."

"It says nothing here about having to tread the parsnips."

"It fills me with 'orror, Bert
— 'aving to stand by an' watch all
that lovely beer go flat!"

"I'll never come home drunk,
I might see two of you."

"I never drink and drive — I
find it slops all over the steering —
wheel."

"He's my greatest achievement,
I made him a millonaire."

"I hate bath-night!"

"If you don't mind me saying so, dearest, your back seat driving CAN be a bit annoying."

"But Mr. Pugh, I always thought lifeboat practice was on deck with everybody there."

"I've told him we're eighty thousand tons and we're still in the port, but all he says is: 'Better be safe than sorry' "

"Back, I say — BACK you mutinous dogs!"

"You need double top for game, Bert!"

"You'd better put your shirt on quick! That's the Admiral's wife!"

"I said I'm sorry — what more do you want?"

"Crow's nest to bridge — the fog's clearing, and we should be seeing the old white cliffs of Dover any time now."

"Not fish AGAIN!"

"On my shoulder, stupid!"

"They won't take a cheque, Gladys – we'll have to go round the Horn!"

"Captain! The swimming pool is leaking!"

"Looks like mutiny, sir."

SEESIK CRUISES
(**TOURIST CLASS**)

"And this is your favourite D.J., Fred Smith, saying goodnight folks, and don't forget to tune in again tomorrow."

"The temperature's rising — we must get them out or it will be too late."

"I wonder what's on the other channel."

"He wants to be the first man to cross the Atlantic by gondola."

"I CAN make her dance, but it gives me hiccups."

"I didn't say you were a stowaway — I just asked to see your ticket."

"I know there's 'Land Ahoy'. There always IS, you twit!"

"Ah, here it is — the signal means 'Heave-to or I . . . .'"

"Let me know when you're smiling."

"I had a parrot once but it bit me!"

"How do yer keep yer feet so soft and white, mate?"

"They say that if you hold one to your ear, you can hear the washing machines!"

" 'Bout time you got your shoes soled."

"Your slip's showing."

"Who left their cuff-links in that shirt, eh?"

"Wait until the neighbours see my new hat!"

"I said, it's a BATMAN suit for you."

"By the way, Grimble, did you know they're pulling down the gasometer?"

"My husband feels a little better but he won't be at the office today!"

"Just something she ran up out of a couple of old salary cheques."

"Good news, sir! We are definitely slimmer round the elbow!"

"What dreamy stockings, Sylvia — it looks JUST as though you're not wearing any at all!"

"That you, tosh? This is ole Charlie-Boy 'ere."

"Personally, I couldn't stand all the noise — "

"We all have a bet on whether or not you have a hole in your sock."

"Could I see something a little less lightweight?"

"Madam has got what we in the trade call 'whackin' great plates of meat' . . . !"

"Thorough, aren't they? I only came in to buy a stud!"

"Stand by for another rotten impression of Maurice Chevalier . . .

"When are you going to mend the holes in me trouser pockets, Gladys?"

"Now, don't forget, sir, on the first stroke of midnight, your trousers will fall down."

"That suit has just about had it, Fred — but then, so have you . . . "

"You never TOLD me one of your arms was shorter than the other."

"I keep getting little stabbing pains in the head, Dora."

"I know it's mink but why do you always have to buy me something USEFUL?"

" . . . dearer materials . . . extra labour-charges . . . "

"You have it on back to front — oh, I don't know though."

"I know just what you're going to say, sir, and I agree with you. The buttons need moving!"

"I want to stop the delivery of a fun fur!"

"What d'you mean, next year's fashions? — The dummies aren't dressed yet!"

"Who was it HE called 'A bit of skirt'?"

"I might have worn it ten years ago, Hilda, when I had a figure like that to show it off!"

"I thought it would go with your mini-car and shorty raincoat."

"I'll try it on and see the wallet reaction."

"It's George tonight so it had better be the non-crush."

"Well, what d'you know? — my first attempt and the length is just right!"

"Henry, it's about time you had your shoes heeled."

"I STILL feel cold!"

"Waist (and it's a new world record) 52!"

"Our Economic Crisis model, sir — no pockets but plenty of flaps."

"Fortunately, sir, turn-ups are in again!"

"It might catch on, but personally I think it's too way out."

"When will you realise this is 1967, Dad?"

"When did we last make you a suit, Mr. Briggsly?"

"The advert said 'A simple unobtrusive gadget that will add ten inches to your height!'"

"Why can't you try and look a little more manly? — more like your sister!"

"Oh . . . that's Isaac Newton, the village idiot."

"Cowardice in the face of the enemy.
How plead ye, Guilty or Not Guilty?"

"It's a demarcation dispute, sire —
between the Sheet Metal Workers and
the Allied Butchery and Slaughterhouse
Union."

"I don't care if you ARE off to the
crusades. I want it back NOW!"

"Nothing to worry about, old chap. Just take two of these tablets after meals and paint a cross on your front door."

"It's not the pay, Sire — I just don't think I'm cut out for the Army."

"Can we have our ball back, please?"

"Psst! Saucy hieroglyphics?"

"You're to be my stooge at the next Command Performance."

"The man's been naughty, darling."

"Do you mind? I'm trying to
get these windows cleaned!"

"Next"

"DO you mind? We were here first!"

"C'mon, Eric! All the best birds'll be gone!"

"Oh Lor — it's a repeat of the programme we saw LAST Christmas."

"It's in perfect condition, Sire — it belonged to a coward!"

"Darling! Our first quarrel!"

"So NOW he decides to be cremated."

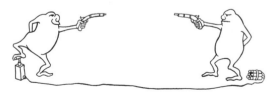

"Come on Julius, we've seen it before."

"How about this one? — Third Crusade — leaving late July — stopping at sun drenched Cyprus, glorious Greece . . . "

"Er — Land ahoy, sir!"

"Step outside and say that again!"

"I think he's just a little bit disappointed with his prize."

"I'm afraid we're running a bit short of slaves, Sire."

" . . . and to think I spent three hours making those meatballs . . . "

"There's been a coup d'etat — I'm to free you, and you're to execute me!"

"O.K., so you've been unluckier than most — is that any reason to quit?"

"I thought it would make a change from blackbirds."

"No, the chap I had in mind isn't a dietician, but he guarantees to knock a few pounds off."

"Quick! Go back before you lose your nerve."

"What's that lazy varlet doing? He should be gathering winter fuel!"

"I hate to tell you this, but Fred Smith got in!"

"Why shouldn't I sing? It's a free country, ain't it?"

"WHERE did you say you got those lions?"

"It started off O.K., then they had one strike after the other . . ."

"If you insist the world IS round when do you suppose we start going downhill?"

"It's fast again . . . !"

"It never reigns but what it paws!"

"Afraid it's no rest for you when you come home, dear!"

"Not swan AGAIN!"

"Ah, ah!—You're peeping!"

"I see old Joe is hanging by his thumbs again, Skipper. Was it something he SAID?"

" . . . and now red you on black me."

"I take it then, Clarence, none of that grub was poisoned?"

"For my next imitation . . . !"

"I have a feeling you do not love me any more, Sir Geoffrey."

"No wonder we're losing, that's 'Come to the Cook House Door'!"

"But I distinctly said 'RABBIT PIE'!"

"By Jiminy — isn't that the new Mark VII with the semi-automatic back sight?"

''After that last fight I've had to change my name to Short John Silver''

"It's a good idea, Watt, but can't you develop it just a little bit?"

"Cor! I'd forgotten it was bath night!"

"Fore!"

" . . . and I expect at least four miles per flunkey."

"And after spending the whole morning at the hairdresser's!"

"If you ask me, a lot of it's faked."

"Who's been resting on my laurels?"

"Just a minute — I'll see if he's in."

"I wouldn't let MY kid go around
with a haircut like that!"

"You looking for a fight?"

"Give in?"

"Well — perhaps just a
teeny, weensy one, then!"

"Okay, okay — heads we ravage the countryside, tails we stay in and have a quiet Sunday at home."

"OTHER way, you!"

"Same old story mate, fancy uniform, pocket fullof money, and a cock and bull yarn about a villa back home."

"Don't buy it, mate . . . it's not an official programme."

"Yes, I could do a party of ten for twelve-and-six per head."

"Haven't you finished ironing my trousers yet?"

"If you ask me, this dictatorship's getting soft!"

"I flogged him the scrap iron rights after the joust."

"Say XCIX."

"Do you really think it's just a harmless phase he's going through?"

"My husband's carrying on with your wife!"

". . . and he'll NEVER apologise first – it's ME who has to do the patching-up."

"I'm afraid my marriage is on the rocks!"

"Why don't 'cher try slappin' 'er across the chops?"

" 'Course, you could always have her beaten up . . . "

"You must control your temper and treat your husband with more respect — bye-bye, dear, I'll be home at the usual time!"

"Of course there will be some dinner for you if you come around, Mother."

"We've been married a year now, Alice, isn't it about time your Ma stopped crying?"

"Oy, Not so fast — there's still something of yours in the bathroom."

"Pa, can I stop annoying granny, now? — I'm getting tired!"

" . . . Your mother!"

"Don't be silly, mother dear, George and I LOVE having you."

"If I thought for a moment that you were smiling!"

"Henry, fetch your hacksaw and make it up with mother."

" . . . about this letter you sent us in 1950, saying you were coming for a week . . . "

"Sorry, mother, I forgot about your headache!"

"Sssh, mother! — Don't keep using the words 'throttle' and 'choke'!"

"How DARE you say my
mother interferes!"

"Mother is very quiet!"

"I'm fed up with having to sleep in
the bath every time your mother
breaks out of jail!"

"We've just got a shocking
telephone bill, Mum
— what are yours
like in Australia?"

"Blimey! Doesn't your mother ever give up?"

"George! Have you read his badges lately?"

"Are you sure the kid's undersealed, dear?"

"It keeps him out of mischief."

"Liven it up a bit — I'm getting sleepy!"

"No! It does NOT say what her statistics were."

"Mother! You don't mean YOU'VE read it too?"

"Dad! There's a cigarette case just like the one Mum gave you in this shop window."

" . . . then they got their decree absolute and lived happily ever after!"

"P'raps I could grow up to be a dumb blonde?"

"Waste? Oh no, my husband gets the nails wholesale."

"Mummy, we had to leave the party early — Mrs. Brown went and shot herself!"

"I'll have to come back later — I've only got five!"

"I'm very good at bird impressions — I eat worms!"

"Stop beefing! I can soon teach him to shave."

"Did you have a nice time at Joan's birthday party, darl . . . !"

"Yes, dear . . . yes, dear . . . yes, dear
. . . yes, dear . . . "

"Yes, I DO know what happens
to little girls who don't eat their porridge
—they grow up to be fashion models."

"Dad can empty it quicker than that!"

"I must say your husband is
very good with children."

"Where did we go wrong, son?"

"I sent Alfie to bed — he'd been fighting again!"

"Good thing we didn't get him the SENIOR chemistry outfit!"

"I think he must be at that interesting age. He's just informed me that Aristotle was a load of old cobblers!"

"Do you HAVE to drag your foot behind you like that?"

"You mean to say you called me in from play, and made me wash my face and hands for THIS?"

"It was smashin', Mum — can I have another party tomorrow?"

"Quick — get this note to the N.S.P.C.C.!"

"He keeps asking me to do it again."

"But, Dad — we're holding a secret meeting!"

"Sis — take your teeth out and make us laugh like the other night."

"Two thousand three hundred and four pieces of coal."

"The suspension seems okay, but I'll want the wheels balanced."

"It doesn't bother ME that you spent two hours in there, but there are OTHERS who would be interested to know!"

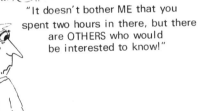

"Other kids are satisfied with a bedtime story!"

"Other boys collect train numbers . . . make models . . . "

"What do you mean, my spelling isn't so good, Dad? — That's my algebra!"

"I don't think he could have read the headlines, do you?"

"Watch for the acceleration past the butcher's — she hasn't paid him this week."

"Daddy took me to the Zoo and an animal came in and paid 20 to one."

"Eureka!"

"That's nothing — MY father can afford to travel by train!"

"The other mothers are demanding
a saliva test . . . "

"Going to say my prayers
— anyone want anything?"

"Heel!"

"That's another lie! I wasn't
expelled — I resigned!"

"These birds and bees — why don't
they use the Pill?"

" . . . and by the way,
I won't be asking
any more of those questions that
embarrassed you!"

"Mum — how long has Dad been short-sighted?"

"He starts school next week — he starts school next week — he starts school next week . . . "

"There now — THAT'S something you can tell your psychiatrist about some day!"

"You can't blame me — you shouldn't have moved."

"Is that Dad shaving or Mum scraping the toast?"

"Does yours talk to you in a sort of foreign language?"

"For goodness' sake put more expression into it — I can't tell Little Red Riding Hood from the wolf!"

"Mummy says I can come to your party if I promise not to eat too much jelly."

"Gosh, Sis! There's another man turning around to admire my Space-suit!"

"I AM sorry, Mrs. Ponsonby, he's never done such a thing at home. But then, we haven't got a piano!"

"Yeah, this is her — that yours?'

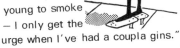

"I know I'm too young to smoke — I only get the urge when I've had a coupla gins."

"Dad, why does ginger-pop spoil my dinner and Martinis give you an appetite?"

"Just try a mouthful, darling — pretend it's mud!"

"Try not to laugh, Mabel — it will only encourage him to be naughty."

"Oh, no! — not MORE violence, Dad!"

"If Daddy's little man must have a story, then Daddy's little man will dam' well stay awake and listen."

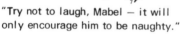

"'You dare to get lost once more,' I said . . . "

"We're playing Mothers and Fathers — care to audition for the lodger part?"

"If I had married Fred Barnsley,
HE'D have taken me somewhere
for holidays."

"What's for breakfast, Ethel?"

"Will you please get rid of this black carpet — I keep losing my socks."

"He can't get used to a bungalow
— every time it rains we get this
performance!"

"Molly! How many kids have we now?"

"What do you mean, you can't find the starter?"

"Why ever did you invite your twin sister round? — You know I hate the sight of her!"

"I've been eating my lunch this way for thirty years — you'll have to be patient, now that I'm retired!"

"When is Mum coming home with our new baby, Dad?"

"In the morning I does a bit o' weight-lifting and punchin' the bag, then she gets up and goes to work."

"And who, pray, suggested you should try your hand at making rum cake?"

" . . . but OUR marriage is going to be different isn't it, darling?"

"Time you cut the grass, dear — it's tickling my back!"

"Er — Happy Birthday, dear."

"You've got money on the brain — you never hear ME keep on about it, do you?"

"She's left me, Uncle Albert."

"I should have known better than to send Frank to get the parrot stuffed!"

"You DID mean it when you said you liked the men in your life to have a sense of humour?"

"Same old routine. Here we go. 'Had a hard day at the office, yes, dear, no, dear, three bags full, dear' — Hey, where's the carpet?"

"I admit I lost the key — but I'd have thought you'd have found an easier way in!"

"Ordinarily I wouldn't give her such a big, expensive gift but this is our Silver Wedding."

"When are you going to mend that tap?"

"Ah! Henry must have got last week's children's crossword right . . . "

"I remember when you used to KISS me goodbye, then it was just a PECK, and now . . . "

"What? And burn myself out by the time I'm seventy?"

"Judy, my wife. She was, of course, a blind date."

"For Pete's sake stop moaning. This isn't the ONLY house with a leaky roof you know!"

" . . . and then we'll go to the chemist to get something for Maria's back."

"He's been reading about this new cold virus!"

"Mildred, this has got to stop! I've nowhere to hang my coat."

"Oh, Emily! You've come back to me after all these years — what's for dinner?"

"Moi woife's 'ad to stop 'elpin' me with the ploughin' — says the 'arness was 'urtin' 'er shoulders!"

"Henry's always been the same — takes a violent dislike to people for no reason at all!"

"Until tomorrow then my little cherry blossom . . . er, I mean, Bert."

"I've got instant indigestion.'

"Now don't get excited — I found them on the bus!"

(a) "I'm leaving you, Ralph!"

(b) "It wasn't an easy decision, believe me."

(c) "Your indifference has driven me to it — your damned indifference."

(d) "Pardon, dear?"

"Er, surely your husband told you about ME, Joe, his identical twin brother?"

"You sure this is the way to grind coffee?"

"Emily! You've got the safety-catch on!"

"You've done something with your hair!"

"Can't we go out for a walk without you worrying about the house being burgled?"

"Of course, I think of you when I'm at the office, silly. Why, only today I said to myself — 'I wonder what old whatsername is cooking for my dinner'!"

"There are others worse off, y'know — supposing you had a splitting 'eadache like the poor woman in this 'ere commercial?"

"Oh, good! She's peeled the potatoes ... "

"Oh, don't apologise for mistaking this for the bank — my wife always does . . . "

"Quick! Where's your cheque book? The bank's getting some more money in."

"I see Maisie's got behind with the milk bill again!"

"I'll say this for them — they're fair!"

"He owes money all round — the TV people, the Gas Board, the Marriage Bureau . . . "

"I don't know how we managed when my hubby was working."

"You're an anonymous donor, I suppose?"

"SOMEONE here owes the petty cash five bob!"

"Mind you pay the electric bill today."

"Every week Henry puts a little by for next year's rates!"

"May I have ten bob to tide me over until you're in a better mood?"

"Jack Lilburn, I never thought you'd go through with this!"

"Now which of you did he know as 'Pussykins'?"

"I'm just about fed up with staying in while you read my endowment policies and bank statements, Fiona . . . "

"I — er — just called to wish you good morning!"

"Your wages got frozen."

"Well, dear, we've finally saved enough coupons to send away for an ashtray — gimme a couple of quid to post 'em."

"In aid of the Tin-Collection-Box-makers' Benevolent Fund, ma'am."

"What was it? — Two bob or half-a-crown?"

"Ah ken it's a new carpet, Duncan, but we'll have tae start walking on it sometime!"

"THAT'S not the way to pay my alimony!"

"According to my records you're bang up to date with A to GLU and GLY to LON, but you're three months in arrears with LOO to TAN and TAO to ZIM."

"My pay slip starts off all right — it's when I get to this perishin' end I'm in trouble."

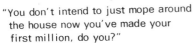

"You don't intend to just mope around the house now you've made your first million, do you?"

"Better not, Junior weighs it every day."

"Mavis! — Is that you?"

"There, dear — 2s. 6d. saved."

"Hurry up, please, I'm double parked!"

"I thought it was the house he meant!"

"Any other reference?"

"It's the Water Rates, dear!"

"I'm a bit worried about old Kinsley!"

"I always thought they lent you money!"

"Thank heavens for that!"

"And one day all this will be yours!"

"Oh dear! Could you reverse to where it was five bob?"

"Funny — I could have sworn a gruff voice said 'Thanks, mate!'"

"Every time you open my door, Mr. Spriggs, there's an awful overdraft."

"I wonder if you could oblige me with a shilling for the gas?"

"He's been a faithful husband — always pays his alimony on time."

"Too generous — that's your trouble, Hobbs!"

"Just how far behind are we on our mortgage, Sidney?"

" . . . and to my wife who always nagged me to save something for a rainy day . . . "

"Good morning, sir — I'm the new rent collector!"

"Too big a risk, Mr. Forster, you're accident prone."

"As you know, your uncle was the scientist who launched our very first Space rocket."

"We just borrowed it over lunchtime, Mr. Gringle. We haven't any matches."

"Care to come and help me spend it, Honeybun?"

"Sometimes I think you're OBSESSED with money!"

"Certainly I'll donate a little something to the new hospital — my husband's brains!"

"That's going to be a tough act to follow, Sis!"

"How about a big kiss, baby? . . . Pass it on."

"I thought it was only tired businessmen that came in here!"

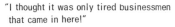

"Miss Smugley, what can we do today to pep up my autobiography?"

"Yes, Ken, but just because it was crowded when we got IN . . . "

"The Insurance Company insists I lock the door and subdue the lights to safeguard my etchings."

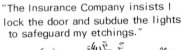

"Is that your peeping Tom or mine?"

"Is that satellite still orbiting in black underwear?"

"I'm so bluesome and alone . . . no man of my own . . . "

"What d'you mean, you'd still love me even if I were only a road-sweeper? We earn jolly good money!"

"Just their OPINIONS, Smith!"

"A tight dress like that must play havoc with the circulation . . . I'm beginning to feel it already."

"Mum's not keen, but I think Dad likes you . . . "

"Boy! If only she were
fifteen years younger!"

"That, I presume, was your wife . . . !"

"I never know what to say to girls —
except that I have a million pounds."

"Well, Barclay, as I
was saying . . . "

"Henry! It's the YOUNG LADY
who's doing the survey!"

"Am I to understand you
disagree with me?"

"You appear to have upset your
drink, sir. Will you permit me to
purchase you another?"

"I'd rather YOU told him
to stop insulting you, dear
you know what a nasty temper I've got."

"Well . . . what do YOU want?"

"Sir, despite our contrasting opinions,
I'm convinced that a combined
effort will enable us to reach
some measure of warm agreement —
to our mutual benefit."

"Steady! It's considered very
dangerous to strike a
chemist with a bottle
of nitroglycerin in his pocket!"

"When I said 'step outside and say that' I didn't mean I was coming too!"

"I'll have the same as the gentleman on my left."

"I can stand just so much abuse . . . then I run like the clappers."

"Don't discuss politics if you can't control yourself."

"Watch your language, Bighead!"   "Are you still angry with me, darling?"

"They won't be out for another hour—we're showing 'Gone with the Wind'."

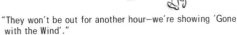

"Pilot to tower! Permission to land?—Permission to land?"

"Probably thought it wasn't worth landing for only two."

"We get a lot of low-flying aircraft around here."

"You're coming in too low, you're coming in too low, you're— ah, forget it!"

"Got the right time on you ol' boy?"

"You'll really have to do something about your weight, Fanshaw!"

"Why couldn't you take my name and address like they do on the buses?"

"That's Digby Carruthers, our new Air Correspondent."

"They must be expecting somebody pretty important."

"Ugh! Here come ironbird — twin-engine turbo-prop by the sound of it."

"I've been wondering how they could do this trip so cheaply!"

"Goodness gracious! How would they cope with a breakdown up HERE?"

"Up a bit, George, we've just missed an archery club."

"It used ta be jest cowpoke versus cowpoke, but now EVERYBODY wants to get in on the act!"

"If'n you wait till somebody moseys along the street I'll give you a demonstration."

"The court will adjourn while the two learned gentlemen shoot it out."

"This is your third last stand in six months, Colonel!"

"At this point in the movies, the US Cavalry come charging over the hill — but THAT'S in the movies."

T

"Goldurned Yankee carpet-baggers are robbin the West of its natural resources!"

"Would you lot mind not doin' thet? — I ain't got a music licence."

"He got the idea from a pitcher he saw **of some** dawg."

"During this chilly weather, Senorita Lucy, one daren't leave a durn thing off."

"We better come a-callin' some other time, Betsy — seems they already got company."

"Like ah said — this place sure is daid Sunday afternoons."

"After ya've had the twins, Martha, hurry up out here an' rustle me up some chow."

"It's amazin' how these Injun scouts kin pick up a trail from jest the smallest clue."

"Ah've had jest about enough o' yore veiled insolence, Ringo!"

MISS LUCY'S CAFE

"Ketchup stains, nuthin'! Thet's genuine hunnerd per cent. blood, stranger."

"The last pianner player left kinda sudden."

"Hi, there, Hank — hear tell ya jest managed to escape from some little bit o' trouble in Dodge City!"

"Ah! There you are Harris — I was beginning to wonder if something had happened to you."

"It ain't the moon the coyotes howl over — it's the shortage of trees."

"You cavalry? US Injuns . . . howdy!"

"Sure it's a FREE election — ya come in the door fer nothin' didn't ya?"

"It's taken you a long time to cover a simple story like an Indian uprising Johnson!"

"Funny — it's only when mother comes for a few days YOU have ta head fer the hills lookin' fer outlaws."

'But, Major! Ah said the Injuns went THAT away!"

"Him not doing War Dance. Him breaking in itchy underwear . . . "

"What'll it be, podner? Regular, Highgrade or Supergallop?"

"Ah say, do away wi' shot-guns fust!"

"Ah never did care much fer discussion groups."

"Naw, stranger, he ain't daid drunk — jest daid."

"Ah'd like ta purchase three 'Git-well' cards."

"Allus the same when 'Frontier Circus' hits town!"

"Aw, stop makin' setch a fuss — anybody'd think I wuz pulling a tooth out, stead o' jest a li'l ole bullet."

" . . . then Red Ridin' Hood reached for her six-gun an' said 'O.K. Grandma make yore play'!"

"Last owner wuz a dame."

"NOW what goldurned excuse has he got fer stoppin'?"

"Me heap glad me not pale-face baby!"

"Jest who do ya think yore callin'
a bunch o' no-good Teds?"

"The service is becoming durn
infrequent these days!"

"230 egg an' chips, 150 steak an' mash, 200 ham an' eggs . . . "

"A fine time YOU'VE picked ta run outa sticking plaster!"

"Ignore him — he's probably drunk!"

"It don't even tell ya how ta hash up a mess o' beans!"

"That could ha' been mighty serious — they might have spilled ya whusky!"

"The Smith and Wesson thirty-eight, I think."

"Sorry — ah'm anti blood-sports."

COME ON OUT RINGO — WE GOT YA SURROUNDED

"Oh! Oh! Ah think th' Sheriff's goofed agin!"

"I didn't know Howling Wolf was throwing a braves' party today."

"There's a hole in something I had to patch today. Let's see, what was it . . . ?"

"Someday, son, all of this will be yours."

"Letter for ya, dear, by Pony Express."

"Aw, give the postman his durned Christmas box and let's have done wi' all this!"

"Do ya think they're expectin' us, dear?"

"Same thing every Sunday mornin' — play-by-play descriptions o' Saturday's gunfights."

"Greetings! — And next time kindly dispense with the twenty arrow salute."

"And what makes you think she's talking to her boy-friend?"

"Hey! I wuz in front of him!"

"Ya ain't losin' a daughter, suh, yore gainin' a six-gun."

"Let's see now . . . six bottles o' whusky, ten busted chairs, two broken winders, three burials . . . "

"Cain't he read anythin' 'sides Goldilocks an' them three goldurned bears?"

"Chief said he wanted heap big POW WOW — not bow-wow!"

"The sky overhead, a saddle for ma pillow, and the prairie for ma bed — what a bum way of gettin' a night's sleep!"

"O.K. — so you ain't rustled no cattle, robbed no banks, or kilt no guys, heck! Nobody's perfect."

"Yeah! An' what makes you so sure he's Bat Masterson?"

"Maybe they jest want to say 'Howdy' "

"Gimme a dime fer an ice, daddy dear, or I'll blow yer goldurned foot off."

"Quit hidin' behind thet badge, Marshal!"

"It ain't the drink ah comes ta this joint fer — it's the company."

"Billy the Kid's in town!"

"Ah'm his manager."

"We're peace-luvin' folk in this here town, Ringo . . . that's why we're gonna pump ya full o' lead."

"This is the 'Meanwhile back at the ranch' bit I was telling you about."

"I think it's in love with my hat!"

"A victory over the palefaces — ANOTHER load of messy old scalps to clutter up the wigwam."

"Stop complainin'! If'n yore cold, pull up another durn bear."

"Say hallo to the nice, paleface, children."

"Blacklegs!"

"I'm giving you 24 hours to git outa town."

"Tumbleweed sure plays his part in openin' up the West."

"Quit doin' thet — Ah keep thinkin' Wyatt is a-comin' in!"

"Ya shouldn't have gone a sun-bathin', Miss Lucy — they think you're one of them now."

"Darn it, McGurk! There ARE other ways of clearin' a space fer yerself at the bar!"

"Yeah? An' what makes ya think ah'm drunk — ya adorable creature?"

"Shortage of women doesn't seem ta bother old Tumbleweed none!"

"Eat yore cereal, if ya want ta grow up fast on the draw like yore Paw."

"Took a thorn outa his foot once — now he won't leave me!"

"O' course — ah'll admit it ain't one of the quietest neighbourhoods in the world."

"Fisby, would you kindly remove those ridiculous transfers?"

"For goodness' sake make up your mind whether or not you want to grow a beard and let's get to bed!"

"Mr. Green – this is Mr. Jones, and Mr. Hobbs."

"I still think a mini-skirt getting out of a mini-car is far more breathtaking."

"Left or right?"

"You're wasting your time, they're probably all watching a film!"

"Sorry, everyone — false alarm!"

"And whose bright idea was it to build a sunken bath?"

"He's wasting his breath — it's closed on Sundays."

"Don't look now, Miss Wilson,
but I fear we have a troublemaker
on our hands."

"Lovely! You can't beat a nice,
old-fashioned imitation log fire!"

"I think they must be putting
something in our tea . . . "

"I hate these sad endings, don't you?"

"I say, Ferguson, wouldn't these make wonderful sleeping bags?"

"It's all very well your complaining, Madam — how do you think I like being on the night shift?"

"I'm sorry about this, lady, but I'm sweating on the firm's Salesman of the Year prize."

"Why don't you pick on somebody your own size?"

"About the ventilator you've just fitted . . . "

"What are you staring at? Clear off!"

"You've been chatting up a tent for the last half-hour!"

"Hurry up, Helen — I can't hold on much longer!"

"How do you spell 'Chapter One'?"

"It's a recipe a friend gave me for making husbands take their wives out to dinner."

"He just threw me some nuts."

"Is it okay if he pays cash, Mr. Wilkins?"

"If she tells us how she was walled up in 1358 just once more I shall SCREAM!"

"They keep very much to themselves. Occasionally they drop in on a Sunday to watch the Epilogue."

"Er, I'm the 'other man'."

"Hey, Mac, is the moon like out then?"

"You're not going out again, are you, Franz?"

"It's ages since we had one of these unsliced loaves."

"When does your pen-pal go home?"

"You'll never guess what I had for lunch today."

"Never mind, dear, I think you're beautiful."

"Nigel! You PROMISED me you'd lay off the dog pills!"

"I'm glad MY husband doesn't do that every morning — she's their maid."

"How do you know you don't like it? You've never had chips and custard before."

"I really must fit that serving hatch with a sliding door!"

"If you ask me, she's getting too big for her boots!"

"This bit here, where the punk puts the bite on the D.A., is YUMMY!"

"I have a question. Do you want cheese or sardines for supper, dear?"

"I say, your Grandfather IS a slow reader, isn't he?"

"Produce 25 Merry Mop Meat Pies and recite the soliloquy from Hamlet and you win ten bob."

"Would you be terribly, awfully angry if I changed my mind and didn't go after all?"

"It's your last chance, Elaine — if anything happens to THIS one, we'll have to put you on to making the tea!"

"Met Arnold through a marriage bureau they'd only just started up, so there wasn't much choice."

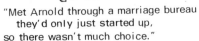

"Out drinking till all hours — coming home half sloshed — football every Saturday — always broke — I just can't keep up with her!"

"Right, Mr. Kamasuki, seventy gross 'I'm Backing Britain' ties, thirty gross 'I'm Backing Britain', hankies, and twelve thousand 'I'm Backing Britain' pens, delivery next week."

"What do you mean you're a 'Don't know'? — I haven't asked you anything yet!"